High Sierra

Wisconsin/Warner Bros. Screenplay Series

High Sierra

Edited with an introduction by

Douglas Gomery

Published for the Wisconsin Center for Film and Theater Research by
The University of Wisconsin Press

Published 1979

The University of Wisconsin Press
114 North Murray Street
Madison, Wisconsin 53715

The University of Wisconsin Press, Ltd.
1 Gower Street
London WC1E 6HA, England

First printing

Printed in the United States of America

For LC CIP information see the colophon

ISBN 0-299-07930-9 cloth; 0-299-07934-1 paper

Publication of this volume has been assisted by a grant from
The Brittingham Fund, Inc.

Contents

Foreword

In donating the Warner Film Library to the Wisconsin Center for Film and Theater Research in 1969, along with the RKO and Monogram film libraries and UA corporate records, United Artists created a truly great resource for the study of American film. Acquired by United Artists in 1957, during a period when the major studios sold off their films for use on television, the Warner library is by far the richest portion of the gift, containing eight hundred sound features, fifteen hundred short subjects, nineteen thousand still negatives, legal files, and press books, in addition to screenplays for the bulk of the Warner Brothers product from 1930 to 1950. For the purposes of this project, the company has granted the Center whatever publication rights it holds to the Warner films. In so doing, UA has provided the Center another opportunity to advance the cause of film scholarship.

Our goal in publishing these Warner Brothers screenplays is to explicate the art of screenwriting during the thirties and forties, the so-called Golden Age of Hollywood. In preparing a critical introduction and annotating the screenplay, the editor of each volume is asked to cover such topics as the development of the screenplay from its source to the final shooting script, differences between the final shooting script and the release print, production information, exploitation and critical reception of the film, its historical importance, its directorial style, and its position within the genre. He is also encouraged to go beyond these guidelines to incorporate supplemental information concerning the studio system of motion picture production.

We could set such an ambitious goal because of the richness of the script files in the Warner Film Library. For many film titles, the files might contain the property (novel, play, short story, or original story idea), research materials, variant drafts of scripts (from story outline to treatment to shooting script), post-production items such as press books and dialogue continuities, and legal records (details of the acquisition of the property, copyright registration, and contracts with actors and directors). Editors of the Wisconsin/Warner Bros. Screenplay Series receive copies of all the materials, along with prints of the films (the most authoritative ones available for reference purposes), to use in preparing the introductions and annotating the final shooting scripts.

In the process of preparing the screenplays for publication, typographical errors were corrected, punctuation and capitalization were modernized, and the format was redesigned to facilitate readability.

Unless otherwise specified, the illustrations are frame enlargements taken from a 35-mm print of the film provided by United Artists.

In theory, the Center should have received the extant scripts of all pre-1951 Warner Brothers productions when the United Artists Collection was established. Recent events, however, have created at least some doubt in this area. Late in 1977, Warners donated collections consisting of the company's production records and distribution records to the University of Southern California and Princeton University respectively. The precise contents of the collections are not known, since at the present time they are not generally open to scholars. To the best of our knowledge, all extant scripts have been considered in the preparation of these volumes. Should any other versions be discovered at a later date, we will recognize them in future printings of any volumes so affected.

Tino Balio
General Editor

Introduction
Reworking the Classic Gangster Film

Douglas Gomery

With the production of *High Sierra* in 1940, Warner Brothers fashioned a new variation of the classic gangster film. This screenplay provides a unique record of one part of its creation. To facilitate the use of the script, I shall analyze the production of the film, then note the major differences among the novel, revised shooting script, and film, and finally survey why modern critics find this film such a significant work. My purpose is not to provide yet another "definitive reading" of the film, but rather to situate, historically and critically, the important document that serves as the focus of this book.

Warners' Production System at Work

Like the four other major studios during the 1930s and 1940s, Warner Brothers engineered a complete system of production, distribution, and exhibition to maximize long-run profits. Senior brother Harry Warner, from the New York office, coordinated distribution, exhibition, and finance. Jack Warner ran the studio-factory in Burbank, California. In order to keep costs low, Jack Warner maintained a strict division of labor for all studio tasks. For this process, Warner continually trained new workers and introduced potential stars to ensure that Warners' movies would remain popular. Jack Warner managed the overall process of stasis and change; his assistant, Hal B. Wallis, handled the day-to-day decisions within Warners' framework. In turn, Wallis placed an associate producer on each major feature film and thus directly monitored all changes and emergencies. Power flowed from the top at Warners; this hierarchy of decision making ensured control of uniformity and maximum cost saving. The production of *High Sierra* illustrates how this system worked when most successful. To initiate any project, Jack Warner and his assistants selected a potential story. In 1940, Warner and Wallis had important reasons to choose W. R. Burnett's forthcoming novel, *High Sierra*. Jack Warner liked authors with good track records. In 1931, Warners had turned Burnett's first novel, *Little Caesar*, into a successful gangster film. Wallis had directly supervised the making of *Little Caesar*. Subsequently, Burnett had provided Warners with two more narratives for motion pictures: *Dark Hazard* (1934), based on his 1933 novel of the same name and remade as *Wine, Women, and Horses* (1937), and *Doctor Socrates* (1935), a gangster story that was remade as *King of the Underworld* (1939).[1]

When the novel *High Sierra* was published in 1940, reviewers in the United States and Great Britain hailed it as a superior piece of gangster fiction, principally because of the portrayal of hero Roy Earle. For *New Republic* critic Max Gissen, the Earle character was "a mixture of old-fashioned decency and sharp rebellion against the average man's role in society." Others compared, quite favorably, this new work to *Little Caesar*. Christopher Barton of the *New Statesman and Nation* (U.K.) argued that "*High Sierra* [will be] another box-office smash for Edward G. [Robinson]. You can almost hear the cameras at work while you read."[2] Still, the novel did not

1. "Warner Brothers," *Fortune*, December 1937, pp. 110–113 ff.; Jack L. Warner, *My First Hundred Years in Hollywood* (New York: Random House, 1965); David Thomson, *A Biographical Dictionary of the Cinema* (London: Secker & Warburg, 1975), pp. 593–94; Richard Corliss, ed., *The Hollywood Screenwriters* (New York: Avon, 1972), pp. 297–98. These footnotes survey the large number of materials concerning *High Sierra* in English. No attempt was made to compile items in other languages.

2. Substantial reviews of the novel *High Sierra* appeared in the following: *New Republic*, April 8, 1940, p. 480; *New Statesman and Nation*, August 3, 1940, pp. 114, 116, 118; *New York Herald Tribune Books*, March 10, 1940, p. 10; *New York Times Book Review*, March 10, 1940, p. 6; *New Yorker*, March 9, 1940, p. 90; *Saturday Review*, March 30, 1940, p. 12; *Spectator*, August 2, 1940, p. 128; *Times Literary Supplement*, July 27, 1940, p. 361. Information on W. R. Burnett was gathered from Stanley J. Kunitz, *Twentieth Century Authors*, first supplement (New York: H. W. Wilson, 1955), p. 149; Harry R. Warfel, *American Novelists of Today* (New York:

make the best seller list as had *Little Caesar*. (Burnett would wait until the early 1950s for his next, and last, best-selling novel, *The Asphalt Jungle*.) Warners purchased the exclusive movie (and broadcasting) rights on March 27, 1940, for twenty-five thousand dollars.

Warner and Wallis immediately set in motion Warners' vast technical staff. Each studio department head contributed to an efficient, cost-minimizing production schedule. The nature of a department's involvement depended on the specific division of labor. The make-up and costume departments provide contrasting examples. Make-up head Perc Westmore receives full credit at the end of *High Sierra*; in fact, he did little of the actual physical labor, instead planning and supervising the work of numerous assistants. On the other hand, costume designer Milo Anderson was directly involved. Anderson specialized in certain stars, one of whom was Ida Lupino. After *They Drive by Night* (1940), *High Sierra* was the second film for this partnership. Anderson and Westmore did have one thing in common: both had been with the studio since the coming of sound, as had most Warners' production employees.[3]

Warner and Wallis also assigned experienced persons to help shoot *High Sierra*, thus guaranteeing trouble-free production. Director of photography Tony Gaudio's career stretched back to movie making's earliest days; by 1911, he had become head cameraman for Carl Laemmle's Independent Motion Picture Company. Gaudio, who came to Warners in the early 1930s, was the consummate studio cameraman—he had no specialty. For example, just before filming *High Sierra*, Gaudio worked on the spectacle *Juarez*, the war film *Dawn Patrol*, and even the Torchy Blane B-series. In 1935, for his craftsmanship on *Anthony Adverse*, Gaudio won Warners' only Academy Award for cinematography

American Book Co., 1951), pp. 64–65; "W. R. Burnett," *Film Dope* (U.K.), July 1974, pp. 49–50; *Hollywood Reporter*, March 18, 1940, p. 4.

3. Jim Bishop, *The Mark Hellinger Story* (New York: Appleton-Century-Crofts, 1952), p. 266; *Motion Picture Herald*, August 10, 1940, p. 27; David Chierichetti, *Hollywood Costume Design* (New York: Harmony, 1976), pp. 74–86; Frank Westmore and Muriel Davidson, *The Westmores of Hollywood* (New York: Berkley Medallion, 1976), pp. 62–77.

for the 1930s. *High Sierra*'s director, Raoul Walsh, also had a long, varied career. Walsh began as an actor in films in 1909, moved behind the camera in 1914, and went on to direct several of the most popular films of the 1920s: *The Thief of Bagdad* (1924), *What Price Glory* (1926), and *Sadie Thompson* (1927). He debuted at Warners in 1939 with *The Roaring Twenties* and remained with the studio until 1951 as one of its most reliable and prolific directors.[4]

Not all those behind the camera had two decades of movie-making experience. For example, associate producer Mark Hellinger and composer Adolph Deutsch had worked at Warners only a short time and would go on to fashion the important part of their careers after they moved to other studios, Hellinger to Universal and Deutsch to MGM. Of the relative newcomers, co-scriptwriter John Huston achieved the most enduring fame. Huston embarked for Hollywood in 1938 (for the second time) to become a contract scriptwriter for Warners. In 1939 he worked on the blockbuster *Juarez* and, during the following years, *Dr. Ehrlich's Magic Bullet* (for which he received an Academy Award nomination). After the success of *High Sierra* and with another Academy Award script nomination for *Sergeant York* in 1941, Huston was permitted to direct as well as write. Huston's first effort was *The Maltese Falcon* (1941). Going on to a career as a director-writer-actor, he won for Warners two Academy Awards (best direction and best original screenplay) for *The Treasure of the Sierra Madre* (1948).[5]

The production of *High Sierra* was unique—and important for

---

4. "Tony Gaudio," *Focus on Film*, January 1973, p. 33; Martin Quigley, ed., *Motion Picture Almanac, 1945–1946* (New York: Quigley, 1946), p. 117; Phil Hardy, ed., *Raoul Walsh* (Colchester, England: Edinburgh Film Festival, 1974), pp. 111–54; Kingsley Canham, *The Hollywood Professionals: Curtiz, Walsh, and Hathaway* (London: Tantivy, 1972), pp. 81–138; Raoul Walsh, *Each Man in His Own Time* (New York: Farrar, Straus and Giroux, 1974).

5. Bishop, *Hellinger*, pp. 267–367; Ted Sennett, *Warner Brothers Presents* (New York: Castle, 1971), pp. 304, 312; Quigley, *Almanac, 1945–1946*, pp. 72, 316; Thomson, *Dictionary*, pp. 232, 461; William F. Nolan, *John Huston: King Rebel* (Los Angeles: Sherbourne, 1965), pp. 37–39; Gerald Pratley, *The Cinema of John Huston* (New York: A. S. Barnes, 1977), pp. 36–37; "John Huston," *Current Biography*, February 1949; Stuart Kaminsky, *John Huston: Maker of Magic* (Boston: Houghton Mifflin, 1978), p. 18.

the Warners studio—because of all the new talent in front of the camera. In 1940, Humphrey Bogart and Ida Lupino were only supporting players; Jack Warner successfully elevated both to star status with *High Sierra*. For Bogart, the official Hollywood legend argues it provided "the break," the major turning point in his career. One of Bogart's numerous biographers, Joe Hyams, summarizes the myth most succinctly:

In 1940, thanks to a fortuitous chain of circumstances, [Bogart] got an important break. George Raft had been offered the role of a gangster in a picture called *High Sierra*. The Hollywood censors decreed that the gangster must die, because he had committed six killings. Raft refused to die in a film. Paul Muni turned it down because it had been offered first to Raft. Cagney declined it, and so did Edward G. Robinson.[6]

The accounts then vary on who pushed for Bogart. Some claim it was Hellinger; most credit Charles Einfeld, Warners' publicity director. More plausibly, Jack Warner moved down to the next name on the list of eligible male stars, and that was Bogart. Yet if *High Sierra* was a turning point in Bogart's career, it was a small one. In truth, with *The Maltese Falcon* Bogart became a major star. That film was released in October 1941, nine months after *High Sierra*.[7]

In 1941, Ida Lupino received top billing for *High Sierra*. Only later with the creation of the "Bogie" myth would the star rankings seem reversed. Born to a noted British stage family, Lupino was brought to Hollywood by Paramount in 1933 (at age fifteen) to become another Clara Bow. She played minor ingenue roles for several studios until she landed a part in *They Drive by Night*. Jack Warner then signed her to a standard seven-year contract and cast her with Bogart, who also had a supporting role in *They Drive by Night*, for her next film, *High Sierra*.[8]

6. Joe Hyams, *Bogie* (New York: New American Library, 1966), p. 68.

7. Ezra Goodman, *Bogey: The Good-Bad Guy* (New York: Lyle Stuart, 1965), pp. 31–32, 194–95; Nathaniel Benchley, *Humphrey Bogart* (Boston: Little Brown, 1975), pp. 64–100. See also Alistair Cooke, *Six Men* (New York: Knopf, 1977), pp. 183–205; Alan Barbour, *Humphrey Bogart* (New York: Pyramid, 1973); Allen Eyles, *Bogart* (London: Macmillan, 1975); "Humphrey Bogart," *Current Biography*, May 1942, pp. 7–8.

8. Jerry Vermilye, "Ida Lupino," *Films in Review*, May 1959, pp. 266–83; "Ida Lupino," *Current Biography*, September 1943, pp. 54–56; Thomson, *Dictionary*, p. 341.

Two new supporting players appeared in *High Sierra*: Arthur Kennedy and Joan Leslie. Both became Warners' staples during the 1940s. A New York legitimate actor, Kennedy came to Warners for *City for Conquest*, released September 1940, and then signed a seven-year Warners' contract. *High Sierra* was his second film under that contract. Although Warners had plans to make Kennedy a star, at this point in his career he continued in the slot of top supporting figure, a function similar to Bogart's position at Warners during the late 1930s. Kennedy went on to a distinguished career in films and television. Joan Leslie, although a newcomer to movies in 1940, had started on the vaudeville stage at age five. She had played in minor (and forgettable) films until her work in *High Sierra*. Then Warners signed her to a seven-year contract and starred her in *Sergeant York* (1941). For the next six years she was Warners' resident girl-next-door.[9]

The minor figures—Henry Hull, Henry Travers, Jerome Cowan, Minna Gombell, Barton MacLane, Donald MacBride, and Willie Best—all portrayed their usual character types. Of them all, only MacLane regularly worked for Warners; the rest free-lanced.[10] In sum, Warner and Wallis did take a chance with the stars for *High Sierra*, but with an experienced technical staff, director, and cinematographer and a familiar set of supporting figures, the two executives minimized risk. If Bogart, Lupino, Kennedy, and Leslie had not proven to be successful, there would have been other films in which to try other combinations of this potential "star material."

Most of *High Sierra* was filmed at Warners' Burbank studio, with some location work done in the Big Bear Lake and Lake Arrowhead area of Southern California. The shooting began during the first week of July 1940 and was completed three months later, right on schedule. Immediately the assembly phase commenced.

9. James Robert Parish and Lennard DeCarl, *Hollywood Players: The Forties* (New Rochelle, N.Y.: Arlington House, 1976), pp. 344–61; "Arthur Kennedy," *Current Biography*, November 1961; Thomson, *Dictionary*, pp. 326–27; Kyle Crichton, "The Strenuous Life," *Collier's*, June 28, 1941, pp. 13, 36; Gladys Hall, "The Love of Three Sisters," *Photoplay*, October 1941, pp. 40–41, 95–97.
10. Cornel Wilde, a major star of the late 1940s, has a small role in *High Sierra*. He would be the film's only minor player to go on to achieve fame.

Warners' music department, under Leo F. Forbstein, and veteran editor Jack Killifer prepared the film for its release, and *High Sierra* opened in New York on January 25, 1941.

Warner Brothers sold the film quite predictably (see figure 1). Advertisements hailed Lupino and Bogart, "the stars whose startling performances in *They Drive by Night* made them Top Box Office Names," and quoted author Burnett ("My story to top *Little Caesar* is *High Sierra*") and director Walsh ("*High Sierra* is the most thrilling and unusual picture I have directed since *What Price Glory*"). The ads further reminded potential filmgoers that Warner Brothers also had produced the earlier gangster hits *Little Caesar* and *Angels with Dirty Faces* (1938). Warners' publicists provided exhibitors with a six-day serial story, rewritten from the movie, reviews for insertion in local newspapers, and ideas for contests and promotions.[11]

High Sierra opened (first run) in America's largest cities through February and March 1941. Gradually—usually as part of a double feature—it played second, third, and subsequent runs. Each run lasted one week, two at the most. In most cases, exhibitors found the film provided excellent business; for example, it fared 25 percent better than normal in Memphis, Louisville, Los Angeles, New York, Seattle, Chicago, and Pittsburgh. In September, *Variety* noted that it was one of the top grossers of the year, no blockbuster, but a very successful film.[12]

The critical reception to *High Sierra* was generally favorable. Trade papers like the *Hollywood Reporter* found the film to be a fine addition to Warners' string of "crime pictures, . . . a gripping drama of great vitality and sustained suspense, as marked for its impressive characterization as its vivid action. It is real entertainment all the way and should do extremely well at the box office."[13]

11. Sennett, *Warner*, p. 306; Quigley, *Almanac, 1945–1946*, p. 104; the following issues of *Motion Picture Herald*: October 5, 1940, pp. 39, 75; October 19, 1940, p. 40; October 30, 1940, p. 61; December 21, 1940, p. 69.

12. The following issues of *Variety*: January 22, 1941, pp. 9–10; January 29, 1941, pp. 8–9; February 5, 1941, p. 11; February 19, 1941, p. 9; February 26, 1941, p. 9; September 3, 1941, p. 24; also Chester B. Bahn, ed., *Film Daily Yearbook, 1942* (New York: Film Daily, 1942), p. 111.

13. *Hollywood Reporter*, January 22, 1941, p. 3; *Motion Picture Herald*, January 25, 1941, p. 50; *Photoplay*, April 1941, p. 114.

Middle-brow publications agreed with the *Time* reviewer who argued, "What makes *High Sierra* something more than a Grade B melodrama is its sensitive delineation of gangster Earle's character."[14] *New York Times* critic Bosley Crowther waxed in his usual overblown style: "We wouldn't know for certain whether the twilight of the American gangster is here. But Warner Brothers, who should know if anybody does, have apparently taken it for granted and, in a solemn Wagnerian mood, are giving that titanic figure a send-off befitting a first-string god in the film called *High Sierra*. . . . It's truly magnificent, that's all."[15] Only *Variety* found the film wanting and hence predicted (incorrectly) only "ok" box-office revenues. Its reviewer argued that there were "too many side issues that clutter up the [story]" and noted the final third of the film was too long.[16]

Thus, in all respects *High Sierra* was a success for Warner Brothers. The film was made efficiently, and on schedule, and generated sizable revenues. Even the risks, trying new talent, turned into successes: the studio had new stars in Bogart and Lupino, and minor personalities in Kennedy and Leslie. Such was the accomplishment that in 1949 Warners released a remake, *Colorado Territory*. Raoul Walsh directed again, and Joel McCrea played the Roy Earle (Bogart) role, and Virginia Mayo the Marie Garson (Lupino) part. Warners retained the original narrative, but reworked it as a western! In 1955, Warners released yet another remake, *I Died a Thousand Times*, in WarnerColor and CinemaScope. Here the studio stuck to the original genre. Jack Palance played Roy Earle, and Shelley Winters, Marie Garson. Clearly, Jack Warner had been very astute in 1940 when he purchased rights to *High Sierra*, for this narrative would be one of the studio's best long-run investments.[17]

14. Reviews in *Time*, February 17, 1941, p. 94, and *New Republic*, February 10, 1941, p. 180 (by Otis Ferguson).

15. *New York Times*, January 25, 1941, p. 11.

16. *Variety*, January 22, 1941, p. 16.

17. Michael B. Druxman, *Make It Again, Sam* (New York: A. S. Barnes, 1975), pp. 69–74; *Motion Picture Herald*, May 21, 1949, p. 4617; *New York Times*, June 25, 1949, p. 8; *New York Times*, November 10, 1955, p. 45; *Variety*, October 12, 1955, p. 22.

Comparing Novel, Screenplay, and Film

For such an important narrative, we would expect to have numerous drafts of the script, as do other titles in the Wisconsin/Warner Bros. Screenplay Series, with which to trace the specific creative changes. In fact, we have only the novel, final revised screenplay (reprinted here), and the film. Moreover, the story is basically the same in the novel, the screenplay, and the film. In each, the central figure, Roy Earle, is first pardoned, then journeys to California, prepares for the robbery of Tropico Springs resort, escapes, and is eventually trapped and killed in the Sierra Mountains. In the process, he meets a young crippled girl, Velma Goodhue, and her family and helps her obtain an operation for her clubfoot. Later she refuses his marriage proposal. Marie Garson, a former dance-hall girl, wins Roy's affection and survives him at the end. But despite these common elements in the three versions, important differences exist, especially in the beginnings and endings, that change *High Sierra* from a novel about Roy Earle, a man who happens to be a gangster, to a gangster film whose hero is Roy Earle.

As the novel begins, Roy Earle is driving across the Nevada-California desert, having just been pardoned from prison. That information is covered in one sentence. For the next seven pages we learn of Roy's thoughts—nostalgic memories of summer days at the swimming hole, Saturday ball games, visits to Aunt Minnie's house, as well as darker images of fights and stabbings. Roy imagines himself as a tall, heavy-shouldered, hard, and muscular man, a "cross between a farmer and a refined gorilla." Thus, immediately, author Burnett has specified the central interest of the novel, the psyche of Roy Earle. The narrative then traces Roy's mental anguish as he struggles to understand a modern, post-Depression world.

The screenplay opens with a classic icon of the gangster film, the first-page headlines of a newspaper declaring public protest to gangster Roy Earle's pardon. Unlike the novel, there is no interest in Roy's thought process. Instead, Roy's past and present behavior is placed, uncompromisingly, in opposition to society's view of correct morality. The narrative enigma becomes: How will this gangster adjust to a post-Depression world, after eight years in jail? He cannot go straight; in order to repay his debt for the fixed pardon, he must engineer one more robbery. Inevitably, convention dictates, this action will lead to Roy's recapture or death. If the classic gangster tale is one of rise and then fall, *High Sierra*'s variation as a screenplay (and film) is just the fall.

To obtain instructions concerning the robbery, Roy contacts Jack Kranmer. Before Roy arrives, Kranmer and his blonde (unnamed) girlfriend argue. She wants to meet the famous Roy Earle, the legendary bandit of the Great Depression. When Roy enters, the first time we meet him in the screenplay, he is old, gray, and pale, possessing none of the brute size Burnett described in the novel. Kranmer's girl is quite disappointed. This gangster is already on the decline; still, he does not give up without a fight. When Kranmer tries to bully him, Roy slaps Kranmer and then abruptly leaves for his journey to California to meet the top man, "Big Mac." Only then does Roy contact his past by visiting the Indiana farm that had been his boyhood home. At first the farm's present tenant, fooled by Roy's new suit and fine car, reasons that Roy represents the local bank and has come to foreclose. Struck by the irony, Roy assures him he has only come to visit (figure 3). Here we are reminded of the classic justification for the gangster: the Robin Hood figure of the Great Depression. Moments later the farmer recognizes Roy and begins to shake. The Depression is over and now this reputed bandit provides a greater threat than any banker. The power of the mass media, suggested by the headline in the first scene of the screenplay and by Kranmer's girlfriend's interest in the gangster-as-celebrity, even reaches into rural America. Discouraged, Roy leaves. *High Sierra*, even in script form, openly acknowledges its genre; the ability of the mass media to create and shape perception becomes an important motif.

Warners began the film with a long scene not found in the screenplay. This new material signifies, even more specifically than the screenplay does, that *High Sierra* falls into the gangster genre. The film opens with a long shot of a capitol building, a symbol of the state's legal authority. Then with a quick montage sequence, we see the governor sign Roy's pardon and the release of one prisoner, seemingly at random[18] (figure 4). Why is this particular man being set free? In one shot we learn the reason (figure 5). This is another "fix"; the iconography of the driver, the car, and Bogart (the gangster figure of so many previous films), all framed in deep space, gives it away. But as soon as we think we "know" the story, Roy Earle acts strangely. He demands to be driven to a nearby park. What type of ex-convict wants to commune with nature immediately upon release from prison? The film lingers on this seeming enigma. First we see Roy's feet in the grass from the same angle and placement as the shot of his feet in prison minutes before. We even have the film's first point-of-view shot, as Roy examines the trees, birds, and sky. He sits down and basks in the idyllic setting (figure 6).

Only then does the film pick up where the screenplay began. In the film, the newspaper headline becomes a transitional device to the scene where Roy meets Kranmer. Then the film matches the screenplay's initial scenes (described above) quite closely. Yet the new beginning sets off the film even more from the novel. The psychology of the novel has completely vanished; the motif of the mass media, so paramount in the screenplay, is now secondary. Warner Brothers has fashioned another gangster film, albeit an inventive one. This gangster, like his predecessors, has compromised the highest reaches of authority and therefore must be recaptured or die. The mass media do not present a distorted image; despite any Good Samaritan deeds or reflections upon nature, Roy Earle remains a dangerous part of the criminal system, a continual threat until the end.

All three versions of *High Sierra* are traditional narratives in which the enigmas established initially are developed and resolved. It is in closure that again major differences among the three stand out most clearly. Thus the novel, which began with Roy's thoughts, ends in the same fashion. As the police chase Roy, the point of view is always with Roy himself as he tries to make

18. The pardon reads Fall Term, 1932–the date when Roy was convicted. The film is set in 1940, as we learn from the license plate on Roy's car.

the best of a tragic situation.[19] Then suddenly, Roy is killed. It is over in only six pages. Despite all his efforts, reflections, and thoughts, Roy could never fit into a modern, almost alien, world. The screenplay has more enigmas to resolve, and thus requires a longer ending. Roy flees to meet girlfriend Marie. In the midst of this action comes closure of the Goodhue subplot. Earlier Roy helped the family, financed Velma's operation, and posed no physical or moral threat. Yet upon learning of Roy's identity as a gangster, the Goodhues are shocked. Legend now outweighs actual experience. The rest of the screenplay then outlines Roy's entrapment and death, yet unlike the novel the point of view has switched to the authorities at the base of the mountain. The major focus becomes the media carnival surrounding the capture, complete with constant radio reports, large crowds, and concessionaires. The screenplay, which opened with a news headline, closes with a repetition of the motif of the pervasive influence of the mass media. Fittingly after Roy is killed, it is a reporter who mutters, *"Sic transit gloria mundi"* (thus passes earthly fame). The gangster story, complete with the mass media complications, is over.

Because of its more complex opening, the film takes even longer to tie together all the narrative strands. Roy flees, but, having given all his money to Marie whom he will meet later, he must, ironically, perform one more robbery (figure 8). The police are called, and in a one-minute Hollywood montage the police use maps, radios, and a system of roadblocks to capture Roy (figure 9). There is no equivalent in the screenplay. Here we have the full scientific apparatus of the state marshaled against this gangster. Authority, so compromised at the opening of the film, now exposes its full force to redeem itself. Consequently, unlike the novel or screenplay, the police immediately spot Roy and begin the chase (figure 10). During this long pursuit, parallel editing isolates the police, never as individuals but simply as a set of automobiles. Roy cannot escape from this technology; he soon comes upon fallen boulders. But what dominates the center frame, that privileged space in the classic Hollywood cinema, is a sign Road

19. In fact, in the novel, W. R. Burnett often describes Roy's tortured dreams. Such torment becomes an important motif for developing Roy's psychic reactions. This motif is reduced to one short sequence in the film (figure 7).

Introduction

Closed. Again Roy is trapped by the forces of the state, here stronger than even the natural boundaries (figure 11).

In the screenplay, the closure of the Goodhue subplot interrupted Roy's flight to the mountains. There is no such sequence in the film. Closure occurred when Roy visited the fully recovered Velma for the last time and became disgusted with the middle-class monster he had helped create (figure 12). Thus, it is the gangster who is sickened by middle-class Americans, completely inverting the action in the screenplay.

Nevertheless, the gangster must die. In the film, the siege functions also as a media spectacle, emphasizing the drama of authority crushing yet another lawbreaker. A radio announcer narrates the eventual ending (figure 13), while authorities contemplate using a squadron of planes to bomb Roy but settle for a single man using a rifle with a telescopic lens. Because of angle and placement, when Roy is killed, the camera is so far away we cannot even tell if it is Roy (figure 14). He left prison anonymously and is killed thusly. Again a reporter declares Earle wasn't much (figure 15), but no Latin phrase here, just a simple summing up—gangsters can never win. The film ends with Marie's asserting that now Roy is truly free (figure 16). Only with death can this gangster find an escape from the crushing material forces that led him to a life of crime.

This analysis of the beginning and end of the novel, screenplay, and film reveals much about the process of creation of *High Sierra*. The novel is the psychological story of Roy Earle, the anachronism. It focuses on his reactions, feelings, and hopes. The scriptwriters restructured the novel into the gangster genre mold. The gangster must pull a final job but cannot escape, trapped partly because of the mass media. For filming, Warners altered the screenplay so *High Sierra* became a classic tale of the fall of the gangster hero. Roy Earle is unique in that he tries to adjust to normal society, but since the power of the state was so compromised at the film's beginning, no amount of good deeds or communing with nature can help. True freedom comes only with death—a bleak prospect foreshadowing the film noir of the late 1940s.

Finally, all three versions concern not only Roy Earle but also

21

his relations with others, particularly two women. In the screen-play and film, the morality of sexual relations is drawn more clearly than in the novel. In both, Roy meets the pure but crippled Velma and is rejected (figures 17, 18, and 19). Only then does he form his alliance with (the wicked) Marie (figure 20). Thus in the film and the screenplay, this subplot with Velma is nearly over *before* the Tropico robbery. The two relationships are posed as alterna-tives and clearly separated. No moral dilemma is involved: Roy's downfall is partly due to rejection by the virginal woman. In the novel, Roy develops his relationship with Marie long before Velma rejects him. Still, the novel should not be thought of as absolutely more complex. In the novel, Velma remains a naive, simple-minded girl, while in the film she becomes, after her operation, an ambitious, clawing woman. Velma is offensive; Marie, with her steadfastness, elicits more of the audience's sympathy. Thus, although the film on the surface appears to provide the usual di-chotomy concerning sex, upon closer inspection the choice is as ambiguous as in the novel.

Recent Evaluation

On the whole, *High Sierra* is a classic narrative film: the use of editing, camerawork, sound, and mise-en-scène follows quite closely those rules of acceptable film making associated with the Hollywood style.[20] There are several flourishes, for example, the use of deep space as Roy leaves jail and the continuous 360-degree pan during the chase up the mountain. But it is not for stylistic reasons that recent critics find *High Sierra* to be an important film; rather, their criteria focus on the level of theme and genre.

There seem to be three categories for praise. First, some critics applaud *High Sierra*'s influences on other cultural artifacts. (Hum-phrey Bogart's continual popularity has guaranteed that few cine-astes have not seen the film either on television, at a film society, or in a revival theater.) Thus, for example, in *Save the Tiger* (1972), a sequence from *High Sierra* is seen in the background, on a tele-

20. For the most complete summary of this classic Hollywood style, see David Bordwell and Kristin Thompson, *Film Art: An Introduction* (Reading, Mass.: Addi-son-Wesley, 1979), chapter 3.

vision set in a bar. The film may even have influenced poets. Critic John L. Simons argues that John Berryman's "Dream Song No. 9" (1969) contains clear references to *High Sierra*. Simons has compared the two works and has explicated how the film influenced the poem.[21]

Other analysts examine films as "reflected" responses to American culture and find *High Sierra* an important work. For instance, Kenneth D. Alley argues that gangsters, alone, made the rich and powerful pay for the great economic collapse of the 1930s.[22] In 1940, however, Alley claims, "the times" called for people to pull together. The outsider, the rebel had become an anachronism. In response, Warner Brothers raised Roy Earle, their new gangster figure, to a position of high tragedy (in an almost classical sense). *High Sierra* represented a nation's farewell to the gangster and the Great Depression. Following the lead of noted critic Robert Warshow, Alley finds this "last" gangster an important, unique hero:

> Roy Earle becomes, finally, a hero of universal significance, betrayed like us all by his judgement, and by his choices. The clichés of the crime film have been raised to cinematic art of a high order. It is no fluke that *High Sierra* boosted Bogart to stardom, for his portrayal of Roy Earle touched some of the deepest springs in the human psyche.[23]

With this interest in *High Sierra* as a gangster film, it is not surprising that a third type of analysis has emerged, one that tries to elevate the film to an important place in the history of that genre. Films about gangsters can be found in the earliest narrative cinema. For example, D. W. Griffith's *The Musketeers of Pig Alley* (1912) portrayed urban crime on an organized scale; what it lacked

21. John L. Simons, "Henry on Bogie: Reality and Romance in 'Dream Song No. 9' and *High Sierra,*" *Literature/Film Quarterly* 5, no. 3 (Summer 1977), pp. 269–71; Bernard F. Dick, *Anatomy of Film* (New York: St. Martin's, 1978), pp. 90–91; Tom Shales, *The American Film Heritage* (Washington: Acropolis, 1972), pp. 100–103; Manny Farber, *Negative Space* (New York: Praeger, 1971), p. 3.

22. Kenneth D. Alley, "*High Sierra*—Swan Song for an Era," *Journal of Popular Film* 5, nos. 3 and 4 (1976), pp. 248–62.

23. Alley, "*High Sierra,*" p. 261. Robert Warshow's famous essay on the gangster film, "The Gangster As Tragic Hero," can be found in his book *The Immediate Experience* (New York: Atheneum, 1970), pp. 127–33.

was that particular, systematic use of the elements of narrative and iconography that we have come to associate with the classic gangster film. Josef von Sternberg's *Underworld* (Paramount, 1927) provides the usual point of origin for the classic period. In a recent article Gerald Peary argues, convincingly, that the 1928 film *The Racket* more correctly serves as the inaugural effort because of its story of the bootleg wars of Chicago and its concern with the rise and fall of a Prohibition gangster, modeled loosely on the actions of Al Capone.

Still a common narrative is not enough; a genre must also manifest similar iconography. For the classic gangster film, this comes with Warner Brothers' *Little Caesar* (1931) and *Public Enemy* (1931), as well as the independently produced *Scarface* (1932). Their popularity guaranteed that Hollywood would and did produce dozens of imitations during the early 1930s. Moral agencies asserted that a new evil force had appeared on motion picture screens. Warners countered with alternatives: *G-Men* (1935) concerned successful FBI suppression of a gang, *Bullets or Ballots* (1936) dealt with gangs being infiltrated by the police, and *Angels with Dirty Faces* (1938) described the social conditions that led to the rise of gangsterism. With the coming of World War II, Hollywood switched to new variations of the crime narrative with the detective film and film noir, and the classic gangster film became one more important referent within the history of American cinema.[24]

The classic gangster film is characterized by certain rigid conventions of narrative and iconography. Andrew Bergman has argued that the dominant story is best labeled a "success tragedy." The gangster hero, from a poor, immigrant background, works his way to the top—outside the law. The narrative enigmas concern his difficulties in this steady advancement to the summit of a criminal organization. He begins in a subordinate position,

---

24. Gerald M. Peary, "'The Racket': A Lost Gangster Classic," *The Velvet Light Trap*, no. 14 (1975), pp. 6–9; Lewis Jacobs, *The Rise of the American Film* (New York: Teachers College Press, 1939), pp. 68–69, 408–410; Colin McArthur, *Underworld USA* (New York: Viking, 1972), pp. 34–42; Jack Shadoian, *Dreams and Dead Ends: The American Gangster/Crime Film* (Cambridge: MIT Press, 1977), pp. 15–58; Arthur Sacks, "An Analysis of the Gangster Movies of the Early Thirties," *The Velvet Light Trap*, no. 1 (1971), pp. 5–11.

lives only for his work, asserts his extraordinary skill at murder, and finally acquires ultimate power. Then, convention dictates, he must die, killed either by the police or a new gangster-hero. The iconography (repeated elements of the mise-en-scène) of this rise and fall are quite familiar. The site for action is the city, principally at night: dark streets, dingy rooming houses, bars with flashing neon signs outside, and garish nightclubs. The gangster skillfully employs modern America's most complex technology to fight and kill (automobiles and guns) and communicate (telephone). Actors such as Edward G. Robinson and Humphrey Bogart best signified the gangster's unique combination of physical coordination and an aged, beat-up face. Countless character actors and actresses reemerge as necessary assistants, gun molls, stool pigeons, and/or strong-armed, sadistic guards. We usually find uneven lighting, either dappled or deeply shadowed. And few do not recognize the prerequisite double-breasted suits and 1920s flappers' dresses. Throughout the 1930s Hollywood told and retold the gangster "success tragedy" with numerous variations and much invention.[25]

Earlier, in comparing the novel, screenplay, and film, I argued that the film *High Sierra* was a classic gangster movie in which we find a unique hero. Critic Jack Shadoian places the film at a pivotal point within the development of the gangster/crime genre because of this portrayal. After *High Sierra* the deviant behavior of the gangster-hero ceases to be the genre's central focus; instead it is society that has become corrupt. Like Kenneth Alley, Shadoian finds Roy Earle to be a dreamer, a man of nature—in short, a positive figure. Thus Shadoian goes on to argue that

[*High Sierra's*] basic structure sticks close to the classic pattern—the rise and fall of a big shot—with this difference: the pattern is inverted. Here it is no rise and all fall, but by falling the hero rises. He does not die squalidly, in a gutter, but nobly, at the foot of a mountain, and his death

25. Andrew Bergman, *We're in the Money: Depression America and Its Films* (New York: New York University Press, 1971), pp. 3–17; Warshow, *The Immediate Experience*, pp. 132–33; Colin McArthur, *Underworld USA*, pp. 23–33; John G. Cawelti, *Adventure, Mystery, and Romance: Formula Stories As Art and Popular Culture* (Chicago: University of Chicago Press, 1976), pp. 60–61.

is equated with freedom. Having transcended the world and the judgements of morality, the classic gangster has achieved the best he could have hoped for.[26]

What made this narrative inversion possible was a more open and flexible generic form. Thus, Shadoian concludes, *High Sierra* signaled the end of the classic gangster film, and the beginning of film noir.[27]

In sum, for several important reasons *High Sierra* deserves our attention. Overall, although Shadoian's work is the most sophisticated of the current critical arguments concerning this film, it must still be judged as only a first step. Presently film history, criticism, and theory are in a state of flux; the old methods are being reviewed and replaced. Much remains to be rethought, especially the terms of analysis for film genre, and film narrative. One need is clear: film scholars must have ready access to the maximum amount of potential primary data. The publication of the revised screenplay for *High Sierra* provides an important step in that direction.

26. Shadoian, *Dreams*, p. 82.
27. Shadoian, *Dreams*, pp. 67–80.

1. *Advertising from the press book for* High Sierra.

2. *Opening title, over the symbolic mountain.*

3. *Roy returns to his boyhood home.*

4. *Roy leaves jail.*

5. *Roy advances to meet Wally.*

6. *Roy at the park.*

7. Marie observes Roy's tortured dreams.

8. Roy's last holdup.

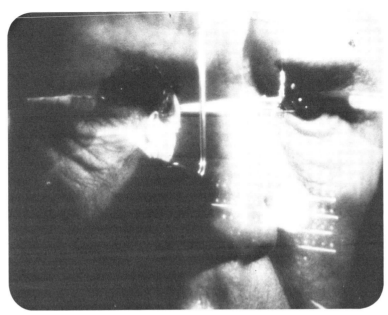

9. The police track Roy (part of the Hollywood montage).

10. The authorities locate Roy.

11. Roy flees up the mountain.

12. Velma has become middle class.

13. A radio announcer reports the drama.

14. Roy is killed.

15. Marie and the sheriff discover Roy's body.

16. Marie understands Roy's death.

17. Roy meets Velma.

18. Roy tries to convince Velma's family to allow the operation.

19. *Velma refuses Roy's proposal of marriage. (Note the movie fan magazine between them.)*

20. *Roy accepts Marie.*

High Sierra

Screenplay

by

JOHN HUSTON

and

W. R. BURNETT

Original Story by

W. R. BURNETT

High Sierra

FADE IN[1]

1. INSERT A BIG HEAD NEWSPAPER CUT OF ROY EARLE at about twenty-six, vitally young, powerful, and rebellious. OVER SCENE comes hot dance music. CAMERA PULLS BACK to include the headline of a Chicago paper.

ROY EARLE, FAMOUS INDIANA
BANK ROBBER, WINS PARDON!

Citizens Protests Ignored

After serving only eight years of a life
term, notorious bandit Roy Earle today
walked out of Mossmoor prison a free
man. Despite the protests of many Better
Business organizations, Earle . . .

CAMERA PULLS BACK TO:

2. MED. SHOT A MAN
hat on, sitting at an imitation mahogany library table with the paper before him. The dance music comes from a radio on the table in a cheap South Chicago apartment. A blowsy blonde leans over his shoulder, staring at the paper. The man takes out his watch:

KRANMER:
He ought to be here. When he comes, get into the bedroom and stay there till he's gone.

WOMAN:
But I want to see him . . .

Kranmer merely glances at her.

WOMAN:
Okay . . . okay.

39

OVER SCENE the SOUND of a car stopping outside.

WOMAN:
Here they are. Wally's brought him.

KRANMER:
Turn that radio off. Then blow . . .

The woman hesitates, starts to say something, then turns off the radio and goes into the bedroom, shutting the door behind her. Kranmer stands up, facing the door.

3.   MED. SHOT   ON DOOR

SHOOTING past Kranmer. The door opens and Roy Earle comes in. Beyond him in the hall, a little nondescript man waves a finger at Kranmer, then quickly closes the door. This Roy Earle differs from his newspaper photo. His hair is streaked with gray, his face is worn and pale.

KRANMER:
Hello, Earle.

ROY:
Where's Big Mac?

KRANMER:
He's gone to California. I'm handling things at this end.

ROY:
Who are you?

KRANMER (extending hand):
I'm Kranmer . . . Jack Kranmer.

ROY (ignoring hand; slowly):
Copper, ain't you?

KRANMER:
Used to be . . . I resigned.

ROY:
I'll bet.

4.   MED. CLOSE SHOT   KRANMER AND ROY

ROY:

>   Since when has Big Mac been teaming up with ex-
>   coppers?

Kranmer scowls, stares at Roy. Roy stares back. The
tenseness is broken by the woman coming back into the
room. She looks at Roy and is shocked by the disparity
between the photograph and the man. Kranmer rises,
turns on her threateningly.

KRANMER:

>   What do you want? Didn't I tell you to . . .

WOMAN:

>   My purse . . . I thought I left it out here . . . I guess
>   I didn't . . .

She takes another look at Roy, then goes hurriedly back
into the bedroom. Kranmer remains standing.

KRANMER (abruptly):

>   Let's get down to business, Earle. Mac wants you to
>   start for California right away. The car downstairs is
>   yours. Here are the keys. (Taking some keys and an
>   envelope out of drawer and handing them to Roy.)
>   And here's your route and some dough. The sooner
>   you get out there, the better.

ROY:

>   What's the setup?

KRANMER:

>   Ever hear of Tropico Springs?[2] It's a resort town . . .
>   richest little town in the world, they call it. The hotel
>   there is some joint! You're going to knock it over.

ROY:

>   Am I, copper?

KRANMER:

>   Look here, Earle, Mac spent a fortune springing you.

You're working for him now. He calls the tune and
you dance to it.

Roy stands up, raises his hand deliberately, slaps Kranmer twice, front and back hand. Kranmer's shoulders
hunch, his little eyes look murder. Roy waits several moments for Kranmer to come for him. Kranmer doesn't.
Roy turns his back on Kranmer and goes out the door.

DISSOLVE TO:

5.   INT. NEW BUICK   CLOSE SHOT   ROY   DAY (PROCESS)
     driving along the highway.

6.   CLOSE SHOT   SIGNPOST
     reading:
                    INDIANA STATE LINE

DISSOLVE TO:

7.   INT. CAR   CLOSE SHOT   ROY   (PROCESS)
     driving along a dirt road. He passes cornfields where the
     corn has been stacked, small farms, cows standing in
     groups under big shade trees. The countryside looks well
     cultivated, very fertile and rich. He pulls up beside a farm
     gate and sits looking at a house that is partly hidden be-
     hind a row of maples. It is a tranquil and beautiful scene.
     A farmer comes down to the fence.

FARMER (with a slight foreign accent):
     Looking for somebody, mister?

ROY:
     Just looking around. This is the old Earle place, ain't
     it?

FARMER:
     Yes. But none of the Earles have been around here for
     five-six years. You from the bank?

ROY:
     No. I used to live around here. Nice country.

CAMERA PULLS BACK as a boy with a fish pole over his shoulder comes down the dusty road, followed by a nondescript dog.

8.   GROUP SHOT   ROY, FARMER, AND BOY

ROY:
> Howdy, son. Any luck?

BOY:
> Not much. (He holds up three small fish that are dangling on a string.)

9.   CLOSE SHOT   ROY

ROY:
> The best place to catch 'em is that hole down below Turner's place. Plenty big catfish in there . . . three-four pounds they go.

The boy looks at Roy as though Roy is cracked.

ROY:
> Used to be anyway a long time ago. Maybe it's fished out.

CAMERA PULLS BACK as the boy looks from Roy to the farmer, who is studying Roy's face.

BOY:
> Three-four pounds . . . Gee!

He turns and goes on down the road.

10.   CLOSE SHOT   FARMER

He is studying Roy's face. A look of horrified recognition slowly comes over his face. He starts back.

FARMER:
> Why . . . Why . . . You're Roy Earle, the bandit!

OVER SCENE the SOUND of the gears engaging and the car driving off. The farmer stares after the car, fright and astonishment in his face.

DISSOLVE TO:

11. LONG SHOT   THE DESERT   DAY
A great, wide, flat expanse vaguely outlined by distant mountains. Chollas and Spanish bayonets cast no shadows. Land and sky are both blinding in the midday sun. A glimmering black road bisects the picture. On the road a car is moving from left to right.

12. MED. PAN SHOT   ROY'S CAR
A mud-splattered Buick coupe traveling at fifty.

13. LONG SHOT   ROAD
SHOOTING through windshield of the car over the shoulder of the driver. The road, which stretches straightaway as far as the eye can see, rushes beneath the radiator.

14. INT. CAR   CLOSE SHOT   ROY EARLE
driving.

15. REVERSE ANGLE
SHOOTING past Roy through the windshield. He overtakes another car, a Model A Ford. As he goes to pass, the Ford swings suddenly to the left.

QUICK CUT TO:

16. A JACKRABBIT
taking a long, slow leap away from the wheels of the cars.

17. MED. PAN SHOT   THE TWO CARS
The Buick turns off the road, bumps over the desert floor.

18. CLOSE SHOT   THE JACKRABBIT
sitting up in the sagebrush.

19. INT. FORD   MED. CLOSE SHOT
    Three pairs of eyes are wide with fright—an old man and
    a girl are in the front seat, and in the rear, an old lady is
    wedged in between bundles, boxes, pots, and pans.

20. PAN SHOT   THE BUICK
    as it turns back onto the road.

21. FULL SHOT   A RUN-DOWN FILLING STATION
    with a single pump and a faded signboard reading:
    "ED'S"
    LAST CHANCE IN FIFTY MILES
    Ed, a tall man in a dirty khaki shirt, stands near the pump
    as Roy drives into scene.

22. EXT. FILLING STATION   MED. SHOT   ED AND ROY

    ED (as Roy turns off motor):
        Howdy, pardner . . . ! What can I do for you?

    ROY:
        Fill her up. She'll take about ten. Take a look at the
        water and oil.

    ED (bustling about):
        Yes, sir, you bet. Hot day, ain't she? Ain't many cars
        coming through right now . . . Little early, I guess.

    Roy, gazing at the distant mountain, doesn't reply. Ed
    looks up, follows Roy's gaze.

    ED:
        You're lookin' at the pride of the Sierras, brother.
        That's Mount Whitney, highest peak in the United
        States . . . 14,501 feet above sea level . . .

    Roy keeps staring, pays no attention to Ed.

    ED:
        I see you got an Illinois license plate . . . You're a
        long way from home, ain't you?

Roy turns, regards Ed with hard eyes. Ed swallows.

ED (weakly):
> You got to excuse me, brother . . . I get lonesome here. When a customer shows up, I guess maybe I talk too much.

ROY:
> Lonesome, eh . . . ? Yeah . . . I imagine a guy would get kinda lonesome out here.

ED (swallows again, looks nervously away, then):
> Look, here comes another car! And brother, is she boiling!

Roy watches the Model A come limping into the station, pull up behind his car. Its radiator cap is off and a jet of white steam is rising three feet in the air. The old man gets out of the car.

PA (triumphantly):
> We made it! (Walks to Roy.) I'd sure like to shake hands with you, sir. Jackrabbit jumped in front of my car and I kinda lost my head. You sure saved our bacon.

Roy has been observing the old man—his patched trousers, suspenders mended with a safety pin, his face covered with a silver stubble, and his clear childlike eyes. Roy's grim face relaxes. Ma, Pa, and Velma are his own kind of people.

ROY:
> Saved my own bacon, too. (Takes the old man's extended hand.) Come far?

PA:
> Clear from Ohio. You?

ROY:
> Chicago.

PA:

> Well, I'm mighty proud to make your acquaintance. You sure can handle a car. Me—I'm kinda shaky at it. Velma—she's my granddaughter—Velma's a good driver—but she gets tired so I won't let her drive too much.

Roy looks toward the Ford.

23.   CLOSE SHOT   VELMA   IN FORD
Smiling slightly, she lowers her eyes. She has a round, almost baby face with small, pretty features and lots of yellow hair tied up with what looks like a candy box ribbon. Although she is twenty years old, dressed as she is, she could pass for much younger, say fifteen. She brings a cheap bag into view, opens it, takes out comb and mirror, and begins to tidy up rather self-consciously.

24.   TWO SHOT   ROY AND PA   FORD IN BACKGROUND
as Roy watches Velma.

PA:

> What's your name, sir?

ROY:

> Collins.

PA:

> Mine's Goodhue . . . Velma—Ma—I'd like you to meet Mr. Collins.

MA (smiling):

> Howdy.

VELMA:

> How do you do.

25.   TWO SHOT   ROY AND VELMA
She starts to put out her hand, hesitates. Roy takes a step toward her, puts his hand out, then lowers it. Roy is ob-

viously impressed by Velma. An awkward moment follows, then:

ROY:
> Pleased to meet you . . . (To Pa.) Well, I guess I'll be on my way.

He hands Ed a bill, turns toward Buick.

ED (running for change):
> Out of five.

26.   MED. CLOSE SHOT   BUICK
as Roy gets in. Pa comes over to the running board.

PA:
> Going far?

ROY:
> Up in the mountains . . . for my health.

PA:
> I thought you looked a little pale . . . Well, I'm going to Los Angeles, God willing. I lost my farm back home. Velma's mother married again and she sorta invited us out. I don't know . . .

Ed comes into picture.

ED (counting it out):
> Two forty-one, three, four, five.

ROY (to Pa):
> I hope you make it all right. (Steps on the starter.) Good-by.

He puts in the clutch, turns the car onto the road. He waves at the Ford. Velma and Ma wave back.

DISSOLVE TO:

27.   LONG SHOT   THE MOUNTAIN
An overwhelming giant with pointed rocky turrets for a

summit. Lordly and mighty it rises over the surrounding mountains.

CAMERA PANS DOWN TO:

28. A STEEP, WINDING ROAD
up which the Buick climbs in second gear.

29. INT. CAR   CLOSE SHOT   ROY   (PROCESS)
driving. The gears whine and stutter. Roy curses them.

30. MED. SHOT   BUICK
as it comes out on a windy plateau. Roy stops at a signpost.

31. CLOSE SHOT   SIGNPOST
It reads:

BROKEN CREEK SUMMIT[3]
Altitude 7,800 Feet

32. CLOSE SHOT   ROY   IN BUICK
He slowly turns his head, witnessing the world around him. His gaze climbs to the mountain, up and up to its summit. He starts, catches his breath.

33. LONG SHOT   THE SUMMIT OF THE MOUNTAIN
CUT BACK TO:

34. CLOSE SHOT   ROY   IN BUICK
looking at the mountain with unblinking eyes. Several moments pass, then he shakes himself, engages the gears, and drives on.

DISSOLVE TO:

35. FULL SHOT   SHAW'S CAMP   EVENING
A handful of cabins and a general store in a grove of pines. The Buick crosses the picture, stops before the store.

36.   EXT. GENERAL STORE   MED. SHOT   BUICK IN
        FOREGROUND
        A Negro, wearing a stocking cap, turns the corner with
        an armful of wood. A little white, smooth-haired terrier
        dog is at his heels.

        ROY:
            Hey, you!

        ALGERNON:
            Yessuh?

        ROY:
            I'm looking for a fellow named Hattery . . . He's
            staying up here . . . him and another fellow.

        ALGERNON:
            They're all in number twelve. Take the first road to
            your left . . . You the party that's expected?

        ROY:
            Yeah.

        ALGERNON:
            Number eleven's your cabin then. Park your car in
            front. I'll drain the water out. Gets mighty cold up
            here nights.

        ROY:
            Okay. (He drives on.)

37.   EXT. CABIN   MED. SHOT
        A tall girl with a long bushy bob and a bold, handsome
        face leans against the front of the cabin, her arms and legs
        crossed, smoking a cigarette. She has on a plaid skirt and
        boots. The Buick pulls into the picture.

        ROY:
            Hattery here?

        MARIE (nods, calls):
            Red . . . Babe . . .

The cabin door opens and a good-looking fellow comes out. He has an irritating air of conceit.

BABE:
> You Roy Earle?

ROY:
> Yeah.

Red Hattery appears. His red hair is coarse and bristly. He has the dented nose and flattened profile of a prize-fighter. His face is covered with freckles. In spite of an engaging grin, he is extremely ugly. He goes up to the car.

RED:
> Hello, Earle. Glad to see you. I can't shake hands . . . I been cleaning fish. Meet my pal, Babe Kozak . . . and this is Marie Garson.

Roy nods shortly.

RED:
> The colored boy's got your cabin all fixed up. You got a cabin to yourself. We was figuring that a big shot like you might be kind of exclusive.

Roy looks the two men up and down, first Babe, then Red, then Babe again. Marie he never gives another glance. Red's grin fades before Roy's scrutiny. He shifts his weight from one foot to the other. Babe, on the other hand, puts an insolent, sardonic smirk on his face and lights a cigarette with as much nonchalance as he can muster. Roy drives up to the doorstep of the next cabin, turns off the motor, alights, opens the rumble seat, lifts out two suitcases, Babe, Red, and Marie watching and exchanging glances.

38.   INT. ROY'S CABIN   FULL SHOT
A room with a cot, two chairs, and a washstand. A curtained door leads into the kitchen. Roy enters with his

bags. Babe, Red, and Marie follow him in. Marie looks into the stove.

MARIE:
All you have to do is throw a match in . . . You sure need a fire up here at night.

BABE:
Yeah . . . you sure do.

ROY (to Babe and Marie):
You two beat it. I want to see Red a minute.

Babe appraises Roy, an impudent grin on his face, then:

BABE:
Okay by me.

He jerks his head for Marie to follow and saunters out. Roy closes the door behind them, then faces Red.

RED (grins sheepishly):
Don't like the idea of the dame, huh?

ROY:
Even guys like you ought to know better.

RED (uncomfortable):
Babe met her in a dime-a-dance joint in L.A. She's strictly okay . . . just sorta looks after things for us.

ROY:
Give her some dough and send her back. Get her out of here tonight . . . Now what's the dope on the job?

RED:
The Tropico season's just startin'. Mendoza—he's our inside man—he says the hotel will be full up in another week. There'll be plenty of rocks in the strongboxes then—plenty.

ROY:
When do I see Mendoza?

RED:

> He'll be up the first day he gets off . . . He's in touch
> with Big Mac, too . . . He'll give you all the news,
> first hand.

ROY (dismissing him):
> Okay.

Red goes to the door, hesitates, fiddles with knob.

RED:

> I want you to know, Mr. Earle, that with you in on
> the job, we feel we're in fast company. I sure heard
> a lot about you. One time, when I was only a kid, I
> seen your picture in the paper, and—

His voice trails off as he sees no friendliness in Roy's face.
Red turns quickly, goes out, as Roy lifts his suitcase onto
the bed and begins to unpack.

39. INT. THE OTHER CABIN   MED. SHOT   MARIE AND BABE
An exact duplicate of Roy's cabin. Marie and Babe sit on
opposite sides of the kitchen table.

BABE:

> Aw, you can have your Roy Earle. What a surprise!
> He's old, and he looks soft around the middle. He
> may be a powerhouse to some people but he's a
> blowed-out fuse to me.

MARIE:

> He's plenty tough, don't worry. Get out of line and
> you'll see.

Red enters, takes a place at the table.

BABE:

> Yeah . . . all right . . . I'll see . . . and let me tell you
> something, you're getting so you just go around ask-
> ing for a smack on the nose. Stop arguing with me
> all the time.

RED (after a pause):
> Boys and girls, I got some bad news for you. Roy says we got to send Marie back to Los Angeles.

BABE (jumps up):
> What? Why, that broken-down . . . I'll . . . I'll tell him . . . (He hesitates.)

MARIE:
> Yeah? Well, here's your chance. You don't want me to go back to L.A., do you, Babe? You go tell him off.

Babe stares for a minute, then sits down.

40. CLOSE SHOT   BABE AND MARIE

BABE:
> I don't know. We need the guy . . . But that's no reason why he should come up here and start pushing us around. (Jumps up again.) Yeah, that's right. He's not the boss no more than we are. He can't—

MARIE:
> Keep it up, Babe; you're going to win this argument.

Babe swings at her with the flat of his hand. She draws back, avoiding the blow. CAMERA PULLS BACK as Red grabs Babe's wrist. Babe winces, tries to pull away.

RED:
> You leave Marie alone. You go smacking her around and I'll cool you off.

BABE:
> Some day I'm going to call your bluff, Red.

RED:
> Call it right now. That'll suit me.

MARIE:
> Cut it out. You won't get nothin' out of fighting but a black eye.

She opens her compact, looks into the mirror.

BABE (to Red):
> I don't care what you or anybody else says, Marie's not going back to L.A.

RED:
> That's what *you* think. He thinks different.

MARIE (applying lipstick):
> I'm not going to be sent back to that dime-a-dance joint if I can help it. (Rising.) I'll go talk to him. I've got an idea.

RED (tiredly):
> With him, I don't think it will work.

Marie looks at him, goes out.

41. INT. ROY'S CABIN   MED. SHOT   DOOR IN BACKGROUND
Roy is sitting at the window, smoking a cigarette, looking out. Through the window the mountain can be plainly seen. There is a light rap at the door.

ROY (calls):
> Yeah?

The door opens. Marie enters, stands for a moment, smiling at Roy.

MARIE:
> Can I see you for a minute, Mr. Earle? Can I sit down?

ROY:
> Help yourself.

MARIE (takes a chair):
> Why do you want to send me back to L.A.? I like it here.

ROY:
> Don't play dumb.

MARIE (significantly):
  I don't intend to. (Roy looks at her as she smiles.)
  Oh, I know what's coming off, all right—and I didn't
  get it from the boys, either. Louis Mendoza told me.
  He talks faster than a horse can trot, and all he does
  is brag . . . So you see, Mr. Earle, Mendoza is the one
  for you to worry about, not me.

ROY:
  I'm not worrying about you. I'm worrying about
  them jitterbugs you've got with you. They'll be
  throwing lead over you before long.

MARIE:
  Oh, I can handle them all right. Babe's tough but he's
  afraid of Red—and I can make Red think my way.

ROY (flatly):
  Got it all figured out, ain't you?

MARIE:
  In a way.

ROY (after a pause):
  Okay. We'll let things go as they are for a few days,
  and see how it works out.

MARIE:
  Oh, thank you, Mr. Earle.

Roy turns away from her, picks up a newspaper. Marie
rises, stands hesitantly beside her chair. Roy glances up,
looks at Marie as though he were surprised to find her
still there. She flashes him a brilliant smile in the best
"come-on" style of a dance hostess.

ROY (in the same flat tone as before):
  Well?

Her smile dims out. Then, after a pause:

MARIE:
Good night.

As she goes out,

FADE OUT

FADE IN

42. INT. ROY'S CABIN   CLOSE SHOT   ROY   DAY
standing before the mirror shaving. Outside is brilliant
sunlight. Birds are singing in a bush by the open window. There is a knock at the door. Roy starts.

ROY:
Yeah?

VOICE (OVER SCENE):
Mornin'. This is me, Algernon.

CAMERA PANS with Roy to the door. He opens it. There
stands the colored boy with his dog.

ALGERNON:
Hello, mister. Anything I can do for you this mornin'?

ROY:
You can rustle me up some breakfast.

ALGERNON:
The lady next door got your breakfast all ready. She
thought I oughta maybe see if you was stirrin' around
. . . yessuh.

ROY (putting on his shirt):
Boy, where did you ever get a name like Algernon?

ALGERNON:
Mah old lady thought it up. Pip, ain't it? Yessuh . . .
it kinda gives me class.

Roy smiles, stoops over, and pets the dog.

ALGERNON:
How you like this dog?

ROY:
Just a dog, ain't he?

ALGERNON (emphatically):
No suh, he's a mighty fine dog, he is. Watch now
. . . Pard! (He turns, looking off toward the lake,
cries.) Ducks . . . ! Ducks!

43.   CLOSE-UP   PARD
as he jumps to attention and raises his ears.

ALGERNON'S VOICE (OVER SCENE):
Down.

The dog drops.

44.   MED. SHOT   ROY, ALGERNON, AND PARD

ALGERNON:
He's a mighty fine animal. Yessuh.

ROY:
Kind of proud of your dog, eh?

ALGERNON:
Oh, he ain't mah dog. He kinda took to me and follows me around. Sometimes I get sort of worried
about it.

ROY:
Why?

ALGERNON:
Well, you see, Pard here, he used to belong to a
woodcutter who stayed up here all the year round.
Well, last winter a snow slide come down. Bam!
Right on this here man's house and killed him. Didn't
kill Pard though . . .

45.   CLOSE SHOT   PARD
looking up at Roy with his head cocked.

46.   MED. SHOT   ROY, ALGERNON, AND PARD

ALGERNON (continuing):
     . . . so a man saw Pard kinda wanderin' around
     lonesomelike in the snow and took him in. Boom
     . . . if that man don't up and die with pneumonia
     . . . a big strappin' man too. So Pard he gets to hang-
     in' around the lodge . . .

47.   MED. CLOSE SHOT   ROY

ALGERNON'S VOICE (continuing):
     . . . and doggone if Mis' Tucker don't come down
     with heart trouble . . . Fell plum over and I hear yes-
     terday she ain't goin' live . . .

48.   CLOSE SHOT   PARD
PAN with Pard as he goes over to Roy and sits up.

49.   MED. CLOSE SHOT   ROY AND PARD
Roy pets him.

ALGERNON'S VOICE (continuing):
     I'm just tellin' you all about Pard in case you want
     him for your own dog.

Marie enters, carrying a tray.

50.   MED. SHOT   ROY, MARIE, ALGERNON, PARD

MARIE:
     Is Algernon breaking your heart with the story of the
     mutt here?

ALGERNON (arranging dishes on the table):
     It's the Lawd's truth!

Roy sits down at the table. Pard ambles over, sits up.

ROY:
     A born panhandler.

He gives Pard a piece of toast. Pard takes it but drops it on the floor.

MARIE:

> Everybody around here stuffs that mutt till it's getting so he won't eat anything but meat.

ALGERNON (laughing):

> That's a fact . . . Well, if there ain't nothin' else I can do for you all, I better be gettin' up to the store. Pard'll stay, won't you Pard?

He leaves, as Roy looks at Marie.

ROY:

> Sit down, have a cigarette or something . . . Where are your boyfriends?

MARIE:

> They're out fishing. That's all they ever do. They never catch anything—but they keep on fishing.

Roy bends over and gives Pard a strip of bacon. Pard only sniffs at it.

MARIE:

> He certainly is spoiled.

Pard looks from one to the other, then solemnly sits up.

ROY:

> He knows we're talking about him.

They both laugh.

ROY:

> Last night I was feeling rotten. This morning I feel okay. Nothing like sleep to set you up.

MARIE (lighting a cigarette):

> What you oughta do is get out in the sun. You're awful pale.

ROY (a short grim laugh):
They didn't let us out in the sunlight where I been stayin' . . . afraid we'd spoil our girlish complexions.

MARIE:
Stir must be awful.

ROY:
Sometimes it's worse than others. Get a mean guard down on you and unless you got plenty of what it takes you might just as well get up on tier number two and jump off. Some of 'em did.

MARIE:
I don't get you.

ROY:
Top row of the cellblock. It's a forty-foot drop and you light on concrete. I seen one guy take the dive. He made quite a splash!

MARIE (wincing):
That's awful!

ROY:
He just couldn't take it. (A short silence.) I was doing the book myself—but I got a break.[4]

MARIE:
How was it—knowing you were in for life . . . ? I should think you'd just go crazy.

51.   CLOSE SHOT   ROY AND MARIE

ROY:
Lots of 'em do. But all I thought about was a crash-out. I tried it once at the prison farm when they moved me out there for good behavior. But the fix slipped and a screw put the blast on me. Yeah—and what was worse, they moved me back behind the big walls. We were just getting ready for another crash-out when I got pardoned.

MARIE:

> I get it. You always hope you can get out. That keeps you going.

ROY (looks at her with interest):

Yeah . . . that's it. You got it.

There is a long silence. Marie and Roy are now definitely interested in each other, and due to this fact a certain awkwardness develops at this point. Marie gets up.

MARIE:

Well, I guess I'll take the dishes back.

ROY:

Thanks for the chow.

Marie grins at him, hesitates, then goes out with the tray. Roy bends over and begins to play with Pard.

DISSOLVE TO:

52.   EXT. GENERAL STORE

Shaw, the camp proprietor, and two fishermen are sitting on the porch drinking soda water and listening to Algernon. The skinny colored boy is playing up to his audience, working for laughs. In the distance the lake glimmers through the trunks of the trees. Roy is walking along a path that leads from the lake.

ALGERNON:

Yessuh, that fellow better fish the banks and watch his step. He better never go out in no boat because that little old dog has put the hex on him for sure.

The men laugh.

FISHERMAN:

Put the evil eye on him, huh?

ALGERNON:

Yessuh . . . the evil eye! That li'l ole dog got the evil eye! His left eye . . . kinda shines in the dark like a cat's eye.

SHAW:
>If it's in the dark, how do you know which eye it is?

Algernon scratches his head. The men laugh.

53.
MED. LONG SHOT   ROY AND PARD
on the road approaching the cabin. Roy throws a stick. Pard is after it like a shot, picks it up, trots back to Roy. Roy pats him, throws the stick again.

54.
INT. CABIN   LOUIS MENDOZA
He is about twenty-five, tall and slender, dressed in polo shirt, V-neck sweater, and slacks. He assumes a superior air and is very proud of his tiny moustache and patent-leather hair. CAMERA PULLS BACK to reveal:

55.
MED. SHOT   AT TABLE   MENDOZA, RED, BABE, AND MARIE
They are playing rummy.

BABE (in a mean mood):
>Come on, Mendoza—are we playin' cards or takin' a nap?

MENDOZA:
>Oh, I am sorry . . . For the moment, my mind was not on the game.

He plays a card. Red grabs it, laughs gleefully.

RED:
>That's for me . . . Thanks, Louis!

BABE:
>Dumb luck, that's all . . . (He plays a card.) Plain dumb luck.

MARIE (playing a card):
>Maybe if you wouldn't squawk so much you'd do better.

Babe glares at Marie. He is about to speak when the door opens and Roy and Pard come in. Louis Mendoza rises.

RED (to Roy):
 This here's Louis Mendoza.

MENDOZA (shaking hands, putting on the charm):
 Delighted, Mr. Earle! (Roy pulls his hand away.)

BABE:
 Sit down, Mendoza . . . sit down. Let's play this hand out.

Mendoza looks at his cards again, plays one. Red pounces on it.

RED:
 That's the baby! (He lays out cards.) Boy! Am I good!

BABE (slams down his cards, jumps up):
 It's just dumb luck. I can't beat dumb luck.

ROY:
 What's it look like at the hotel, Mendoza? How soon do we go?

MENDOZA:
 It won't be long now. (Takes a paper out of his pocket.) This is the layout.

56. INSERT INK-DRAWN MAP (JUST A FLASH)
 on a sheet of paper with the letterhead of the Tropico Springs Hotel, showing the position of the hotel, etc.

BACK TO SCENE:
 Roy studies it. Red looks over his shoulder.

RED:
 I don't know. Babe and I kinda figured our best get-away was over the pass. Nobody'd ever expect us to cross the Sierras to get into L.A.

MENDOZA:
> Suppose it would blow up a sudden storm? If the pass got blocked up with snow, then what?

RED:
> Yeah, that's right.

MENDOZA (to Roy):
> I went in to see Big Mac yesterday . . . He wants to see you, Earle.

57.   CLOSE SHOT   BABE
squatting on the floor, fooling with Pard. He begins to rub the little dog's ears.

ROY'S VOICE (OVER SCENE):
> I'll have a look at the Springs tomorrow. Then I'll drive on in and see Mac.

58.   MED. SHOT   GROUP   ROY IN FOREGROUND
watching Babe and the dog out of the corner of his eye. Suddenly Pard cries out with pain. Babe laughs, doesn't let him go. Roy, moving quickly, kicks Babe's feet from under him, and Babe sits down heavily.

ROY:
> Let the dog alone.

Babe springs up with a murderous light in his eyes but hesitates. Roy's face is hard as flint, and he is carrying his hands loosely ready for a crushing blow.

59.   CLOSE-UP   MARIE
watching with a peculiar expression on her face.

60.   CLOSE-UP   LOUIS MENDOZA   RED IN BACKGROUND
clearing his throat and fussing with his sweater. Red, standing behind him, grins uncertainly.

61.   CLOSE SHOT   ROY AND BABE   OTHERS IN BACKGROUND
        Babe's eyes lower. Roy has stared him down.

        BABE:
            I was just rubbing his ears, that's all.

62.   CLOSE-UP   PARD
        sitting in the corner, his pale, shrewd little eyes fixed on
        Roy. CAMERA PULLS BACK from Pard in time to see Babe
        turn away from Roy.

63.   MED. SHOT   GROUP

        ROY:
            You got licked playing cards and you took it out on
            the dog. I seen you.

        There is a long silence.[5]

        RED (snaps his fingers):
            I almost forgot. Mendoza brought us a present and,
            Roy, I guess you're the engineer.

        He disappears into a bedroom, comes out with a suitcase.
        None of the others has changed position. Red opens the
        suitcase, Roy looks into it. We do not see the gun.

        RED:
            Okay, Roy?

        MENDOZA:
            Big Mac gave me the gun. Know how to work it? Red
            don't and neither does Babe.

        RED (laughing):
            That's a good one.

        MENDOZA:
            What's so funny?

        RED (mimicking Mendoza):
            Does he know how to work it!

66

Roy sits down, calmly directs his speech at Mendoza.

ROY:

> That gun reminds me of one time about nine or ten
> years ago. We were getting ready to do a bank job in
> Iowa. One of the guys had the shakes. We got word
> that this guy with the shakes had talked too much
> and that a bunch of coppers are laying for us down
> at the bank. Nobody says nothing, but Lefty Jackson
> gets out his gun. He sits down and holds it in his lap.
> The boy with the shakes is sitting across the room
> from him. (Roy indicates Mendoza.) Pretty soon Lefty
> just touched the gun a little. It went tut-tut quick-like
> that . . . The rat fell out of his chair dead. We drove
> off and left him there.

64.   CLOSE-UP   ROY

ROY:
Yeah. The gun just went tut-tut like that.

CAMERA PULLS BACK TO:

65.   MED. SHOT   GROUP

Red and Babe stare at each other uneasily. Marie smiles
slightly, glances at Mendoza, who looks worried.

MENDOZA (nervously):
I ought to be starting back. I'm on duty at eight-
thirty.

ROY (slowly):
What's your stunt, Mendoza? You stick right through
the whole job, don't you?

MENDOZA:
Oh, sure. I'll stay right behind the desk and act like
I'm scared. When you fellows get through, I'll call
the police. (Laughs rather weakly.)

ROY:
We don't want no slipups . . . Well, I guess I'll be
hitting the hay.

MARIE:
Don't you want to play some cards?

ROY:
No. (He goes out, followed by Pard.)

RED (after a pause):
Boys and girls, I'm beginning to get the idea our boy friend is no cream puff . . . How'd you like the little bedtime story about the gun that went tut-tut? Did you all get the idea of that story?

MENDOZA (nervously):
Do . . . do you suppose he meant it that way?

MARIE (smiling slightly and glancing at Babe and Red):
Try talking and find out.

FADE OUT

FADE IN

66.   LONG SHOT   TROPICO SPRINGS HOTEL
White stucco walls gleam among the tall palm trees on an immense lawn. Smartly dressed people are protected from the hot sun by big canvas beach umbrellas. People on horseback can be seen. Now and then men and women dressed in practically nothing pass on bicycles. Roy drives up in the Buick.

67.   CLOSE SHOT   ROY
behind the wheel of the car. He folds Mendoza's map, puts it into his pocket, opens the door of the car.

68.   FULL SHOT   HOTEL ENTRANCE
A little group in tennis togs are babbling away.

AD LIBS:
Celia and I are going for a swim. I want a drink. Me for a shower.

Roy enters scene, pauses, looks with awe at the almost naked slender women and girls, then enters the lobby.

69. INT. LOBBY MED. FULL SHOT
huge, dark, and cool looking. CAMERA PANS Roy across
the lobby to the cigar counter.

ROY (to girl):
Cigarettes. (He points, then fishes in his pocket for
change, puts fifteen cents on counter.)

GIRL:
Twenty-five cents, please.

Roy puts down another dime and looks slowly around the
lobby. He sees Mendoza behind the desk. He is giving a
key to one of the men in tennis togs.

70. CLOSE SHOT MENDOZA
who glances up, starts slightly.

CAMERA PULLS BACK TO:

71. MED. LONG SHOT ROY MENDOZA IN FOREGROUND
Roy lights a cigarette, then turns and goes out the way he
came in. A man enters the picture.

MAN (to Mendoza):
Anything in three sixteen?

MENDOZA (after a pause):
Th-th-three six-sixteen . . . did you say?

72. MED. SHOT ROY'S BUICK
Roy enters the scene and gets into his car. CAMERA PANS
with him as he drives slowly along the palm-bordered
drive in front of which is a huge plaza parked almost
solid with shiny cars.

73. MED. LONG SHOT TROPICO SPRINGS
SHOOTING through the windshield, Roy in foreground
driving, his back to CAMERA. He turns from the Plaza into
a narrow road that leads through the driveway onto the
main street. People on the sidewalk call and wave at other
people, who call and wave back.

AD LIBS:
> See you tonight. Going to Jimmy's? Did you get your swim? Badminton this afternoon. Okay.

OVER SCENE the SOUND of a grinding crash of metal against metal. Halfway up the block an automobile accident has occurred. People begin to gather—bicycle riders, pedestrians. Traffic is interrupted. Roy pulls over to the curb, gets out, and walks to the edge of the crowd.

74.   FULL SHOT   THE CROWD
A Model A Ford stands crosswise in the street. Water is pouring from underneath it, flooding the pavement. One fender is crumpled. Three men are pushing a big cream-colored car over to the curb. It has a broken headlight and a lot of scratches on its immaculate body.

MAN:
> Yeah . . . people with cars like that don't care how they drive. They got no money and they got no insurance. It's murder.

ANOTHER MAN:
> Tough luck, Pfiffer.

PFIFFER (a dark-faced little man in white polo shirt):
> He's just an old dodo or I'd take it out of his hide.
> CAMERA MOVES UP TO:

75.   CENTER OF CROWD
There stands a familiar figure—Pa Goodhue. His coat is off. He looks exhausted and bewildered.

ANOTHER MAN (to Pa):
> You know you weren't driving, Pop. The girl was driving. I was standing right over there on the sidewalk. I saw everything.

PA (stubbornly):
> I was . . . I was . . .

Ma Goodhue is sitting in the back seat, bewildered. From the front seat Velma stares defiantly, but soon puts her head down and begins to cry.

76.   CLOSE SHOT   ROY   IN CROWD
staring.

MAN:
What's an outfit like that doing in Tropico anyway?

ROY:
It's a state road, ain't it?

MAN:
I . . . I suppose it is.

PAN with Roy as he pushes to center of crowd.

77.   MED. SHOT   CROWD   PA, ROY, AND PFIFFER IN
FOREGROUND

ROY:
What's wrong, Pa?

The old man gives a gasp, his stare of bewilderment changes to an expression of joy.

PA:
I guess . . . well, I guess . . .

ROY (touching his hat):
Hello, Ma. Don't you worry. We'll get things fixed up.

He glances at Velma, who is wiping tears from her eyes.

PFIFFER (to Roy):
Friends of yours?

ROY:
Yeah . . . why?

PFIFFER:
Just wondered. I know I've got no chance to collect but I'm just curious. I pull out from the curb and wham! I get it. Look at my car.

ROY:
Pa says you didn't make no signal. Talk about collecting, you be careful or you might have to pay off.

PFIFFER:
> A wise guy in our midst, eh? All right, have it your own way. I'll just write the whole thing off to experience.

OVER SCENE the scream of a siren. A radio car pulls up to the curb. A policeman gets out, pushes his way through the crowd.

POLICEMAN:
> What's the matter, Mr. Pfiffer?

PFIFFER:
> I got clipped, but I'm satisfied as long as this guy is.

POLICEMAN:
> Well, if Mr. Pfiffer's satisfied, I am. All right, people, break it up.

78. CLOSE SHOT   PFIFFER, ROY, POLICEMAN

ROY:
> Listen. These people got no dough. They're trying to get to Los Angeles. That car is all they got.

PFIFFER:
> Stop it. You're breaking my heart.

ROY:
> Fifty dollars wouldn't mean much to you.

POLICEMAN:
> Don't you do it, Mr. Pfiffer. They tell me the girl was driving and she's crippled. See? She just got out . . . shouldn't be driving.

79. MED. SHOT   PA, MA, AND VELMA
Pa is leading Ma and Velma to the curb. Velma walks with great difficulty. One leg is shorter than the other or else she has a clubfoot.

80. CLOSE SHOT   VELMA'S FEET AND LEGS
The sole of her right shoe is two inches thick.

81. MED. CLOSE SHOT   ROY, PFIFFER, AND POLICEMAN
Roy is staring at Velma. He is so shocked that he pays no
attention when Pfiffer turns and walks away.

82. CLOSE-UP   ROY
who can hardly believe his eyes.

POLICEMAN'S VOICE (OVER SCENE):
Banging into a brand new car, then trying to put the
chisel on the owner!

Roy doesn't seem to hear him.

DISSOLVE TO:

83. FULL SHOT   AUTO COURT   NIGHT
The moonlight is so bright it casts shadows.

CAMERA MOVES UP TO:

84. MED. CLOSE SHOT   PA AND ROY
sitting under a tree in front of the cabin. OVER SCENE the
SOUND of dishes being washed and now and then the
voices of Ma and Velma. Pa puffs away at his pipe.

ROY:
Pa, how did you ever happen to end up in Tropico?
Get off the road?

PA:
No . . . it was Velma's fault. She had read about it in
one of them smart set magazines. She was dead set
on seein' it . . . poor pet. She was gawking around
looking at things and smacked right into that feller's
car. (After a pause.) I sure was surprised when he
give you that hundred dollars to give me.

ROY (embarrassed):
Don't worry about him, Pa. He's probably got plenty.

PA:
It's the second time you saved our lives, son. When
Velma smashed into that car, I had thirteen cents in
my pocket and a five-dollar bill in my shoe. Of course,
the women didn't know and don't you tell 'em.

73

Roy laughs. It's a real laugh and another Roy.

ROY:
>   Pa, you're all right.

PA (winks):
>   Two of a kind, that's us . . . You know, Roy, I'd never
>   pick you for a big city feller. You said you was from
>   Chicago, didn't you?

ROY:
>   I came out here from Chicago but I'm really from
>   Brookfield, Indiana . . . born there, went to school
>   there.

PA:
>   Little town?

ROY:
>   Yep. My folks had a farm.

PA (striking his thigh):
>   I knew it. I told Ma out there in the desert you was
>   our kind. Matter of fact, you look sorta like the
>   Goodhues; same kind of stock, I guess.

ROY (awkwardly):
>   Excuse me, Pa. I guess it's none of my business, but
>   what's the matter with Velma's foot?

PA:
>   It's a clubfoot. She was born that way.

ROY:
>   Can't nothing be done about it?

PA:
>   One time a doctor told us we could get her operated
>   on but Mabel's so scary . . . Mabel's my daughter.
>   She carried on so we didn't do anything. Last few
>   years I been so broke we couldn't if we'd wanted to.

85.   ANOTHER ANGLE   ON DOOR OF CABIN
as Ma and Velma come out. Velma has changed into a

checked housedress; her thick blonde hair is nicely combed and tied with a white ribbon.

CAMERA PULLS BACK TO:

86. MED. FULL SHOT   GROUP

Roy stands up as Ma and Velma come down the steps. Velma smiles shyly at Roy.

MA:

> We hurried with the dishes 'cause we knew Pa'd be talking your ear off. Pa sure can talk.

They sit down on the grass. After a short silence:

VELMA:

> Look at the stars. I never knew there were so many stars in the sky. Back home you couldn't see them like that.[6]

Roy looks up, then points to the zenith.

ROY:

> See that bright blue star up there? That's Vega. See how it sparkles? It's in kind of a lopsided square with points running up . . . see it? That's the constellation Lyra.

VELMA:

> I see it. How do you know?

ROY:

> A man I used to know, a pal of mine, learned me all about the sky. (Awkwardly.) There wasn't much else to do where we was.

VELMA:

> Is that star always up there like that?

ROY (both proud and ashamed of his knowledge):

> No . . . you see different stars at different times. They change with the seasons. See that other bright star sorta northeast of Vega? That's Deneb in the constellation Cygnus, I think. I'm getting kind of rusty.

VELMA (pointing):

> That big star farther south? You know what it is?

75

87.   MED. CLOSE SHOT   FAVORING ROY AND VELMA
Roy comes closer to Velma to better see the way she is
pointing.

ROY:

> Where? Oh, yeah . . . I think maybe that must be
> Altair. Yes, I guess it is Altair.

Velma's face is upward, her hair falls back. Roy looks at
it. Their hands meet. They stand holding hands.

88.   CLOSE SHOT   THEIR HANDS

VELMA'S VOICE (OVER SCENE):

> They've got such pretty names. I never, never did see
> so many. It makes you dizzy just to look at them.

ROY'S VOICE (OVER SCENE):

> Yeah . . . This feller I was speaking about says at
> night sometimes when he looks at the stars he can
> feel the motion of the earth. Just like a little ball turn-
> ing through the night, with us hanging on to it.

89.   MED. CLOSE SHOT   GROUP

PA:

> Roy, that sounds like poetry, or something. I'm sur-
> prised at you. (He laughs.)

VELMA:

> Grandpa, you be still. It was nice.

Velma and Roy glance at each other. She takes her hand
away, and there is a moment of awkwardness. After a
pause, Roy comes to himself.

ROY:

> Say, I've got to be on my way. I got a long drive ahead
> of me. Got a business date in L.A. . . . . I sure enjoyed
> that dinner. It reminded me of when I was a boy
> back in Indiana.

PA:

> And we sure enjoy your company. I give you that

address, Roy. Now don't you fail to look us up. We
might get lonesome, especially Velma. Some night
you come and take Velma to a movie.

VELMA:

Why Grandpa! You mustn't say things like that!
Maybe he doesn't like movies and anyway why
should he take me? I'm surprised at you.

MA (to Pa):

I declare to goodness, the older you get, the sillier
you act.

PA (laughs, hits Roy on the back):

Roy understands me. Roy and I are old-timers.

ROY:

Well, good night everybody.

PA:

Good night, Roy.

PAN with Roy as he walks toward his car. They watch him
go.

PA:

Fine feller, all right. (With one eye on Velma.) Lucky
girl who gets him.

MA:

Now, Pa, don't you go saying things.

OVER SCENE the SOUND of Roy starting his car.

ROY (calling OVER SCENE):

Good night.

The SOUND of the engine dies away.

PA:

Yes, siree! He's the salt of the earth . . .

90. CLOSE SHOT   ROY   IN CAR
driving, picking up speed.

DISSOLVE TO:

91.   EXT. BERLAND ARMS APARTMENTS   FULL SHOT   NIGHT
        Roy's car comes into view, stops. He gets out and enters
        the building.

92.   INT. HALLWAY OUTSIDE APARTMENT 12   CLOSE SHOT   ROY
        knocking on door. OVER SCENE a man's high-pitched voice
        calls:

        VOICE:
            Come in.

        Roy opens the door, enters.

93.   INT. PARLOR
        as Roy enters from the hallway. It is dark but there is a
        light in the bedroom beyond.

94.   INT. BEDROOM   MED. CLOSE SHOT   BIG MAC
        propped up in bed on several pillows. He is an enormous
        man. His stomach makes a dome beneath the bedclothes.
        There is a quart of bourbon on the night table. As Roy
        comes into the bedroom, Mac's face lights up in genuine
        friendliness. He lays aside a racing form and extends his
        hand. Roy grins.

        MAC:
            Hello, Roy, old-timer! You're a sight for sore eyes.

        ROY:
            Hello, Mac, old boy. Sure am glad to see you. Thanks
            for the spring. I was just getting ready for another
            crash-out. Boy, it was good news!

        MAC:
            Sit down, sit down. Let me look at you. Yep, the
            same old Roy . . . (he hesitates) well, practically. None
            of us getting any younger, eh, Roy?

        ROY:
            No. I don't feel so young anymore.

        MAC (sighs):
            You and me both.

ROY:

What's the matter, Mac?

MAC:

I don't know . . . I can't eat . . . I just ain't hungry . . . and I can't sleep . . . Doc Banton says it's my past life catching up with me.

ROY:

Doc Banton? Is he out here now?

MAC:

Yeah . . . he's runnin' some kind of a phony health service under a phony name. (Slight pause.) Well, Roy, how does it look . . . what do you say?

ROY:

I can't see nothin' wrong with it. If the boys don't blow up on me, it's in the bag. But, Mac, it's goin' to make a big noise in the newspapers. What a joint that is!

Mac laughs and the big dome shakes under the covers.

MAC:

How do you like your helpers?

ROY:

Mendoza's no good. The girl's the best man of the lot. Red's all right too, but dumb. Babe Kozak's a bad one.

MAC:

You say there's a girl? (Angrily.) The chumps!

ROY:

Take my word for it, she's all right.

MAC:

Well, that's your headache, not mine. The glass . . . that's all I'm interested in. Look, Roy, when you get your mitts on it, keep your mitts on it. Deliver it right here. If you're hot, telephone . . . This caper means a lot to me. I spent a pile of dough setting it up and I'm in deep . . . so don't let me down, Roy.

ROY:

> I never let nobody down.

MAC:

> I know. I know. I been dealing with so many screw-balls lately . . . young twerps, soda jerkers, and jit-terbugs, it's a relief just to talk to a guy like you. Yeah, all the real A1 guys are gone . . . dead or in Alcatraz. You're about the only regular left. (He pauses.) I wish I had four like you, Roy. This knock-over would be just a waltz. Yeah, times have sure changed.

ROY:

> Yeah, sometimes I feel like I don't know what it's all about any more.

MAC (absorbed in his own thoughts):

> Yeah, times have sure changed. (He lights a cigar, takes one puff, puts the cigar down.)

ROY:

> What's wrong, Mac?

MAC:

> I don't know. Nothing sets well with me any more. I'm getting so I don't even like bourbon . . . much. (A pause.)

ROY:

> Say, Mac, I don't like that guy I met in Chicago. He tried to handle me like I was a ten-cent heist guy.

MAC:

> Kranmer? Oh, he's new. Used to be a pretty tough copper. Don't worry. He's all right.

ROY:

> A copper's a copper.

OVER SCENE the SOUND of the door buzzer.

MAC:

> Come in . . . That you, Doc?

He hides the bottle of bourbon under the mattress as the door opens and Doc Banton enters.

DOC:
>Evening, Mac.

MAC (jerking his thumb at Roy):
>Look who's here.

ROY:
>Hello, Doc.

It's a moment before Doc Banton recognizes Roy. Then his face shows real pleasure. Doc has heavy white eyebrows and pale, piercing gray eyes.

DOC:
>Well, I'll be . . . Roy Earle, the old boy himself! (Shakes hands warmly.) Last time I saw you was when I took slugs out of Lefty Jackson's chest.

ROY:
>That's right.

DOC:
>Those were the times! Aren't many of the old bunch left . . .

MAC:
>Cut it out, will ya?

ROY:
>Mac tells me you're doing all right.

DOC (taking Mac's pulse):
>Roy, this is the land of milk and honey for the health racket. Every woman in California thinks she's too fat or too thin or too something. If I had come out here in the first place, I'd be a pillar of respectability now. I wish I was thirty years younger. In ten years I'll be a rich man . . . I'll also be seventy. (He puts the ends of the stethoscope in his ears and bends over Big Mac.) Life's a funny thing, isn't it? When

you get what you want, you either don't want it any
longer or it doesn't do you any good. (He listens for
several moments, then puts the stethoscope back into
the side pocket of his coat, rises, then very briskly.)
Same medicine . . . same dosage. Need a new pre-
scription? (Holds up the bottle.) No . . . Good night,
Mac.

As he picks up his bag and goes out, Roy follows him
into the next room.

95.   INT. LIVING ROOM   MED. SHOT   DOC AND ROY

DOC (in a low voice):

> He's in a bad way, old Mac . . . bum ticker, kidneys
> on the blink . . . bad stomach . . . like a kid's toy
> that's running down. (Laughs.) I try to keep him
> from drinking but there's just no stopping old Mac.
> He'll do just as he's always done. Well, maybe he's
> right.

ROY:

> Doc, there's something I want to ask you.

DOC:

> Sure, Roy.

ROY:

> Can anything be done about a clubfoot?

DOC:

> Some of them can be operated, some can't. Why?

ROY:

> A good friend of mine has got a granddaughter.
> She's a mighty nice girl. One time a doctor told the
> old man an operation would fix her up, but they
> didn't do anything about it. I was just won-
> derin' . . .

DOC:

> Young kid, is she?

ROY:

> Well, she's about twenty, I guess.

DOC (winking):
> Twenty. Oh, I see . . . Well, my advice, Roy, is to forget all about her foot.

ROY (slowly):
> Look, Doc, I'm not kiddin' . . .

DOC (uncomfortably):
> I'll have to see it.

ROY:
> Will you go take a look at it, Doc, that is, if I can talk her into it?

DOC:
> Certainly, Roy. You understand I can't do any operating but I can tell you who to go to. It'll cost you, though.

ROY:
> Okay, Doc, I'll give you a ring.

DOC:
> You do that, I'll make you a present of my fee . . . for old times' sake. Good night.

He goes out.

96.   INT. BEDROOM   MED. SHOT
as Roy returns. Big Mac has his glasses on, is writing with a fountain pen on a tablet, glances up at Roy, then goes back to his writing. Finally he tears the sheet out of the tablet, blows on it, then folds it, puts it into an envelope, licks the flap.

MAC:
> There. I feel better now. That's the works. If anything should happen to me, just read this letter and you'll know what to do.

Roy takes the letter. Big Mac reaches for the bottle, pours himself a drink.

MAC:

> Doc says if I don't lay off this stuff it'll kill me, but
> I'm going to die anyway. So are you. So are we all.
> (Raising his glass.) Your health, Roy!

FADE OUT

FADE IN

97. FULL SHOT   UNPAVED STREET
lined with little frame houses, gray, neglected looking.
The Buick drives slowly into the picture.

98. INT. CAR   CLOSE SHOT   ROY AND DOC

ROY:

> Twenty-two eleven . . . the number is.

DOC (grunting with distaste):

> What a neighborhood!

ROY:

> I spoke to the old man over the phone. He thought it
> was a good idea. He's probably talked the rest of 'em
> into it by now. Twenty-two eleven . . . here we are.

99. EXT. HOUSE   FULL SHOT
identical in character to all the other houses on the street.
A curtain at the window is drawn back. Pa looks out, sees
Roy, grins, then disappears. Roy and Doc walk up the
narrow walk toward the house.

100. MED. SHOT   FRONT DOOR
as it opens and Pa comes out on the porch.

PA:

> Hello, Roy . . . Come in . . . Come in. (In a lower
> voice.) I think I got Velma on my side. Mabel, her
> ma, is against us but . . .

ROY:

> Pa, this is Doc . . . Mr. Parker of the Nu-Health In-
> stitute. He's kind of an expert . . . knows his stuff.

PA:

> Proud to know you, Mr. Parker. Come inside.

They enter the house.

101. INT. PARLOR FULL SHOT

A little dingy box of a room. Ma, Velma's mother, and her stepfather stand. Velma stays seated. Mrs. Baughman, Velma's mother, is a faded woman with a peevish face. Her husband, Carl Baughman, is a big man with a thick-set body, bald head.

PA:

> Roy, this is Mabel and this is her husband, Carl.

ROY:

> And this is Mr. Parker.

MRS. BAUGHMAN:

> You say *Mr.* Parker? Isn't he even a doctor

PA:

> He's a specialist . . . personal friend of Roy's.

BAUGHMAN (to his wife):

> Seems to me you'd be thankful somebody is tryin' to do something for that girl of yours.

MRS. BAUGHMAN:

> You got nothing to say, Carl. She's my girl and I'm thinking if he isn't even a doctor . . .

BAUGHMAN (raises his voice):

> He can look, can't he? That won't hurt nothing.

MRS. BAUGHMAN:

> I don't think Velma wants him to look . . . (sweetly) do you, dear?

VELMA (trying to hide her face):

> Pa wants me to . . . so does Roy.

MRS. BAUGHMAN:

> Funny thing to me . . . I never heard of this Roy, and

yet on account of him you're going to let a stranger look at your foot when you won't hardly let me look at it. Who is this Roy, anyway?

PA (growing agitation):
   I told you about him, Mabel . . .

MA:
   If it hadn't been for him . . .

MRS. BAUGHMAN:
   I heard all that but why did he go to so much trouble to help strangers? He musta had some reason.

BAUGHMAN:
   Maybe he likes Velma . . . And you better thank heaven he does. She's past twenty and not married yet and not likely to be. If you want my opinion . . .

102.   CLOSE-UP   VELMA
She is about to cry.

MRS. BAUGHMAN'S VOICE (OVER SCENE):
   We don't want your opinion. Look, you got Velma all upset talking that way . . .

103.   CLOSE SHOT   MRS. BAUGHMAN   OTHERS IN BACKGROUND

MRS. BAUGHMAN (continuing):
   . . . Don't you worry, honey, if you don't want him to look at your foot, you don't have to.

VELMA (tearfully):
   But I do.

104.   FULL SHOT   GROUP

MRS. BAUGHMAN:
   Well, if the child's made up her mind, I'll say no more. Only I don't see . . . all right . . . step in here, Mr. Parker. Come on, Ma.

She flounces out of the room, Velma, Doc, and Ma following. Immediately the SOUND of a door slamming.

86

PA:

> Roy . . .

ROY:

> Yes, Pa?

PA:

> If this here specialist says Velma can be operated on, then what? Operations cost money.

ROY (embarrassed):

> I'll . . . I'll loan you the money, Pa.

PA:

> I could never pay it back. You know that Roy.

ROY:

> I'm not going to worry about that money, Pa.

PA:

> I know . . . Anybody with eyes in his head . . . (Smiles.) Purdy, ain't she? And just as sweet as she is purdy.

ROY (deep breath):

> Yeah.

PA (after a pause):

> Are you figgerin' on marrying Velma, Roy?

ROY:

> I ain't got that far in my figuring.

PA:

> I don't know what's the right thing to do but seems to me before you go puttin' out money, I ought to tell you about Velma.

ROY (slowly):

> What about her, Pa?

PA:

> Well . . . (he hesitates) she's got a feller back home. (He glances at Roy, who is impassive). Yes, sir, it was

funny. Velma's shy, as you can see, and on account she's crippled she used to stay by herself most of the time. But all of a sudden she was running in to Barrowville every day . . . to the library . . . to the movies, and pretty soon I find out she's got a feller. His name's Preiser. He's about thirty years old . . . lost his wife. He's in the insurance business and doing well, but I didn't like it. Velma wasn't happy. I got worried. It was a big responsibility for Ma and me. Nothing seemed to happen, so Ma and me brought Velma out here to her mother. Poor pet, she was awful upset . . . still is. (He glances at Roy, who is impassive as before.) Now, I don't know much about women, Roy, but my guess is Velma's hard-hit and she'll keep on thinking about that feller. (He hesitates.) That's about all there is to it. Maybe it was wrong to tell you . . . but, well, we're old-timers, Roy. We both believe in fair dealing.[7]

ROY (strangely):
Yeah . . . yeah . . .

PA:
I hope you aren't sore or anything, Roy.

ROY:
I ain't sore at nobody.

VELMA'S VOICE (calls OVER SCENE):
Oh—Pa . . . Roy . . .

ROY:
And don't you ever let Velma find out you told me anything.

PA:
You mean . . .?

Velma, almost hysterical with excitement, comes into room, followed by Doc, Ma, and Mrs. Baughman.

VELMA:

> Roy! He says it can be fixed! He says in a little while I can walk as good as anybody.

PA (slapping his thigh, cries):

> Dust my buttons! Do you hear that, Ma? Ain't that wonderful? (To Velma.) Honey, you just thank Roy. Roy's the one. He thought up the whole thing, and he's lending me the money.

MRS. BAUGHMAN (incredulously):

> You? Mr. Collins? You? I . . . I never . . . well . . . I hope you'll excuse the way I acted . . . but I been so worried about Velma. Poor child! After all, I'm her mother and . . .

ROY:

> Mr. Parker here will make all the arrangements. (Goes over to Velma, takes her hand.) You got nothing to worry about, Velma.

VELMA:

> You're so good, Roy. Pa thinks you're the best man that ever lived and I guess Pa's right.

ROY (awkwardly):

> Well, good-by.

He turns abruptly, goes out, his face shining.

PA (mutters):

> Derndest fellow! (Scratches his head.) Derndest fellow!

DISSOLVE TO:

105.   CLOSE SHOT   ROY AND DOC   IN ROY'S CAR   (PROCESS)

DOC:

> It's criminal that nothing's ever been done for that girl before. Simple enough operation. I've got an in with the best surgeon in town. The whole thing will set you back about four hundred. Satisfied?

ROY:
> Sure . . . I'm satisfied. (His face shining.)

DOC:
> But, Roy . . .

ROY:
> Yeah . . .

DOC:
> I'll give it to you straight. You're just putting your neck out. She's not your kind . . . and you know it, Roy. She's going to throw a fit when she finds out what kind of a guy you really are.

ROY:
> Yeah . . . that's right.

DOC:
> You may catch lead any minute, Roy. What you need is a fast young filly you can keep moving with. (There is a short silence.) You know what Johnny said about guys like you and him, don't you? He said you were just rushing toward death . . . Yeah, rushing toward death!

> DISSOLVE TO:

106.   MED. SHOT   SHAW'S CAMP   NIGHT
EXT. CABINS NO. 11 AND NO. 12
as Roy's car comes up the dirt road, stops, and Roy gets out. Both cabins are dark. There is a sharp bark from the corner of the cabin, then Pard runs toward him. Roy bends over to pet the little dog.

ROY:
> What's the matter, pal? Been hiding out?

Certain now that it is Roy, Pard goes into a frenzy of delight. Suddenly Roy freezes. His cabin door is opening an inch at a time. Roy jumps back quickly and makes for the side of the cabin. Pard, following at his heels, barks and yelps.

MARIE'S VOICE (OVER SCENE):
> That you, Roy?

ROY:
> Oh, Marie . . . Say, you had me scared. I thought somebody was layin' for me. What's the idea?

MARIE:
> Pard with you?

ROY:
> Yeah.

MARIE:
> Come on in.

107. INT. ROY'S CABIN   MED. SHOT   MARIE AND ROY
Marie switches on the light as Roy enters. He looks at her in surprise. Marie's left eye is surrounded by a swollen, purplish bruise. There is a gash in her chin, which she has painted with iodine.

MARIE:
> I'm glad Pard's all right. I thought maybe Babe killed him.

ROY:
> Did Babe give you that shiner?

MARIE:
> Yeah. He went crazy. Red tried to cool him off but Babe got hold of a poker and hit Red over the head with it. When Red was down, Babe swung at me twice.

ROY (grimly):
> Were them guys fightin' over you?

MARIE:
> Red was standing up for me.

ROY:
> When was all this?

MARIE:
About dark.

ROY:
Where are they?

MARIE:
As soon as Babe knocked Red cold, he got in the car but the keys were in Red's pocket so he jumped out and started running. I could hear Pard barking and Babe threw the poker at him. Then I didn't hear Pard any more and I got worried. But Red got up pretty soon and staggered around awhile. Then he got a gun and . . . that's the last I saw of them. I ran over here and locked myself in. (She opens the drawer in the kitchen table and takes out Roy's .45.) I found this under your pillow. I figured if Babe sneaked back I could hold him off. He was like a crazy man.

Roy takes the revolver from her, puts it in the waistband of his trousers.

ROY (harsh, vindictive):
You stay here. I'll be back. I'm going out and get them guys.

MARIE:
Take it easy, Roy. You'll get yourself in a jam. Anyway, poor Red—I . . .

ROY:
Shut up and lock the door behind me.

He goes out.

108.   EXT. SHAW'S GENERAL STORE   NIGHT
From within comes the SOUND of a mechanical victrola playing a plaintive Hawaiian tune. Across the road in the shadows, a man leans against a telegraph pole. Roy enters the scene from the foreground, sees the man, stops, slips the gun out of his waistband, and goes quickly toward him.

109. MED. SHOT   RED AND ROY
as Red turns at the SOUND of Roy's footsteps.

RED (gasps):
 Roy!

Roy jams the muzzle of his gun against Red's stomach.

RED (grunts weakly):
 Wait . . . don't . . . please, Roy, let me talk to you a
 minute.

ROY:
 Where's Babe?

RED:
 In the store over there with the fishermen. He's scared
 to come out.

Roy frisks Red, takes his gun away from him.

ROY:
 You was goin' to bump him off, huh?

RED:
 Well, he . . .

ROY:
 I thought so.

RED:
 Yeah, Roy, but . . .

ROY:
 You stay right here.

RED:
 Yeah . . . sure . . .

Roy crosses the street toward the store.

110. INT. SHAW'S GENERAL STORE   MED. SHOT
Babe and a half dozen men are lounging around in front
of the wood stove, smoking and talking.

FISHERMAN:
>He was hooked good and he was played out but just as I was reaching for the net—

Roy enters. At the SOUND of the door opening, Babe looks around. Seeing Roy, he rises immediately.

BABE (pale and shaky):
>Well, good night, fellows. Here's my pal. I guess I'll get along.

A FISHERMAN:
>Good night, son. Hope you get a ten-pounder tomorrow.

BABE (with a sickly grin):
>Yeah . . . thanks.

He joins Roy, who takes his arm, draws him outside.

111.   EXT. STORE   CLOSE SHOT   ROY AND BABE

ROY (as they exit):
>You stinkin' rat!

BABE (swallowing hard):
>Yeah . . . I know. I went crazy. Marie, she . . .

ROY:
>Blame it on the dame.

BABE:
>Look out. (He jumps sideways.) There's Red. He's gunnin' for me.

ROY:
>I took care of him.

BABE (going limp):
>Thanks, Roy . . . thanks. He'da knocked me over for sure if you hadn't . . .

112.   MED. SHOT   THE THREE   RED IN FOREGROUND
Roy pushes Babe over to where Red is standing.

ROY:
> Go on.

113.   TRUCKING SHOT   THE THREE
as they march down the road, Red and Babe in front of
Roy, not looking at each other. When they pass the last
light and are heading toward the dark shadows of the
pine trees, they begin to lag. Roy kicks them in turn, then
prods them forward with the muzzle of the .45.

114.   INT. CABIN   MED. SHOT   MARIE AND PARD
Marie is bathing her eyes and Pard is watching her with
cocked head. He whines.

ROY'S VOICE (calls OVER SCENE):
> Marie!

Marie opens the door. Roy, Red, and Babe enter.

ROY:
> Here he is Marie. Swing on him. Mark him up. Hit
> him with anything you can find. (Picks up a stick of
> firewood.) Use this.

Marie takes it. Hot anger shows in her face as she faces
Babe, then dies out.

MARIE:
> No . . . I don't want to hurt him. (Drops the
> firewood.)

Roy's face is ugly and brutal. He knocks Babe down.

ROY:
> I ain't gonna let him get away with blacking your
> eye.

Babe gets up hastily, badly scared, and Roy starts after
him again. Marie runs to Roy and grabs his arm.

MARIE:
> Don't, Roy! Let him go. He won't act like that again.

ROY (after a silence):
>All right. (To Babe and Red.) Your car's right outside. If I was you, I'd beat it and quick, both of you.

RED:
>Look, Roy, we been counting on this job. We . . .

ROY:
>I'm giving you your chance to blow. If you decide to stick, I'll shoot the first one that don't do what I tell him.

RED:
>Okay, Roy, we get you. Come on, Babe.

They go out quickly. Roy sits down, tosses his gun on the table. Pard comes over and licks his hand. Roy begins to rub the little dog's ears absentmindedly.

MARIE (finally):
>I'm not going back to my cabin, Roy.

ROY:
>No, you better not. The trouble would just start all over again. I'll send you home tomorrow. You can get a bus into Ballard and then take the train.

MARIE (hastily):
>I found a cot in the woodshed. I can fix it up and sleep here in the kitchen.

ROY (without looking at her):
>Okay.

> DISSOLVE TO:

115. INT. ROY'S CABIN   CLOSE SHOT   ON ROY   NIGHT
asleep in bed. Pard is at his feet. Roy turns restlessly in his sleep. Suddenly he flings out an arm, cries in a strange, muffled voice:

ROY:
>Roma . . . is that you, Roma?

116. INT. KITCHEN   MED. CLOSE SHOT   MARIE
awakened by Roy's cry. She sits up in bed, listens.

ROY'S VOICE (OVER SCENE):
>   Roma . . . It's me . . . Roy. I'm Roy . . . Roy Earle.

Marie gets out of bed, holds back the curtains that separate the room, looks at Roy. Pard raises his head, stares at her.

ROY (incoherently):
>   Wait, Roma . . . Wait . . . Look . . . It's me, Roma.[8]

He mumbles a few more incoherent words. Marie stands watching. In a little while she gets back into bed. Outside an owl hoots.

117.   CLOSE SHOT   MARIE
as she reacts to Roy's speeches,

                                                    FADE OUT

FADE IN

118.   INT. ROY'S BEDROOM   CLOSE SHOT   MORNING
ROY AND PARD   IN BED
Pard is digging into the bedcovers after an imaginary squirrel. Roy opens his eyes, sits up in bed. Bright sunlight is streaming in. Roy grins, grabs Pard, flings him gently. Immediately Pard is back for more, growling in mock viciousness.

119.   MED. CLOSE SHOT
as the door to the cabin opens and Marie enters. She keeps the left side of her face turned away from him so that he cannot see the bruises.

MARIE:
>   Roy, Red and Babe are outside. They want to know if it's okay for them to go fishing.

ROY:
>   Sure . . . why not?

MARIE:
>   They act like a couple of school kids. You sure taught 'em a lesson last night.

120. EXT. ROY'S CABIN   MED. SHOT   BABE AND RED
standing a few feet off, rods in hand. Marie looks out of
the cabin door.

MARIE:
> Roy says it's okay. (She starts to close the door.)

BABE (very subdued):
> How's your eye this morning Marie?

MARIE:
> Better, I guess.

BABE:
> That's good.

121. INT. ROY'S CABIN   MED. SHOT
as Marie closes the door. Roy is sitting up in bed smoking
a cigarette.

ROY:
> What's the time?

MARIE:
> A little after eight . . . You musta dreamed hard last
> night. You were sure talking in your sleep.

ROY (quickly):
> I was? What did I say?

MARIE:
> I guess it was somebody's name . . . sounded like
> you called Roma about half a dozen times . . . Know
> anybody named Roma?

ROY (slowly):
> I used to a long time ago . . . funny I ain't thought
> of her in years.

MARIE:
> Who was she?

ROY:
> A little girl. We was kids together in Indiana . . .
> Roma Stover. Their land was next to ours.
>
> CAMERA MOVES TO:

122. CLOSE-UP ROY

ROY (continuing):
She was a towhead. Her hair was awful thick. She tied it up with a ribbon.

123. CLOSE SHOT MARIE AND ROY

MARIE:
Was she your sweetheart? I mean, your childhood sweetheart?

ROY:
Yeah—I guess so. Summer evenings we used to swing on the big gate and the other kids would yell things at us. (After a pause.) She died. She was only fifteen. (Another pause.) Sure is funny . . . me dreaming about her.

Marie looks at him queerly.

MARIE (finally):
I'll make some breakfast for us.

ROY:
Okay.

She goes into the kitchen. Roy reaches for his shirt.[9]

DISSOLVE TO:

124. MED. CLOSE SHOT BREAKFAST TABLE ROY, MARIE, AND PARD
Breakfast is finished. They are sitting across the table from each other. Pard is at Roy's feet.

MARIE:
More coffee?

He holds out his cup and she pours.

ROY:
Well—are you all packed?

MARIE (frowns slightly):
Roy, I thought maybe . . .

ROY:
I'll run you over to Ballard and you can catch the bus.

MARIE:
I haven't got a soul in Los Angeles.

ROY:
Where are you from, Marie?

MARIE:
'Frisco.

ROY:
Your family there? (She nods.) Maybe I can stake you to a ticket.

MARIE:
Roy, remember what you were saying about stir? About the way you kept from going crazy by thinking all the time about a crash-out?

ROY (puzzled):
Yeah.

MARIE:
Well, it's the same with me. I been trying to crash out all my life . . . My old man used to get drunk a couple of times a week and kick us around. My old lady would stand it but not me. I waited for my chance and beat it. I crashed out—just like you did.

ROY (slowly):
Yeah . . . I get you.

125.   CLOSE-UP   MARIE

MARIE:
I came down to L.A. and got a job in a dime-a-dance joint. It was a living but I got pretty sick of being

pawed over, so when Babe came along I crashed out again. I thought Babe was a right guy . . .

126.   MED. SHOT MARIE AND ROY

MARIE (continuing):
  . . . I guess I was never really hooked up with any guys that wasn't wrong so I had nothing to go by . . . till I met you.

She looks at Roy with a flicker of hope in her eyes but Roy only drags on his cigarette. Finally, she rises, stacks the dishes, carries them into the kitchen.

MARIE:
  I'll get ready.

Roy remains at the table smoking. Pard sits at his knee. Roy strokes Pard's head. OVER SCENE the SOUNDS Marie makes moving around in the kitchen. Roy drinks the last of his coffee, drops the end of his cigarette into the cup, then rises, takes his coat down from the hanger, puts it on. Pard watches him with cocked head. Roy picks up his hat. A SOUND, as if someone whispering, comes from the kitchen. Pard's ears pick up. He trots across the floor to investigate. Roy listens, frowns, then goes to the kitchen door.

127.   INT. KITCHEN MED. SHOT MARIE
She has slipped down to the floor in a sitting position, leaning on the cot, her head resting on her arms so that her face is hidden. Her shoulders are shaking. A suitcase is on the cot, open, half packed. Pard tries to push his nose under Marie's arm and get at her face.

ROY (coming forward):
  Marie!

He leans over, tries to uncover her face, but she resists.

ROY:
  Marie! What's the matter?

Pard finds an opening, licks her face frantically.

MARIE (between sobs):
> Stop, Pard.

Roy, sitting on the bed, turns her face to his. It is streaked with mascara.

ROY:
> What's the matter, Marie?

MARIE:
> I want to die . . . I'm no good . . . nobody wants me . . .

Pard is still trying to lick her face. She takes the dog in her arms.

MARIE:
> I guess I just got no friends . . . like Pard here . . . He's got you now but pretty soon you'll be going away. (She puts Pard aside and throws her arms around Roy's neck.) Don't take me back to Los Angeles. Let me stay, Roy. I want to be with you. Please, Roy, please! (Puts her mouth to his but he pulls away.)

ROY:
> Listen to me, Marie. I'm giving it to you straight. I've got plans . . . see? And there's no room for you in them. You couldn't ever mean nothin' to me . . . nothing special, that is . . . You understand . . . ?

Marie pulls his head down. They kiss.

FADE OUT

FADE IN

128. INT. BABE AND RED'S CABIN
Babe, Red, and Marie are playing cards. Roy is walking the floor.

ROY:
> I don't think this business is ever going to come off. I got an idea Mendoza is stalling.

RED:
> Come on, Roy, take a hand.

ROY:
> I don't like it. If the blowoff don't come pretty soon, I'm out.

RED:
> How about playing a hand?

ROY (irritated):
> I don't want to play cards.

Roy goes over to the window, looks out. The others play silently. Roy turns finally.

ROY:
> Tell you what. I'm going to run down to L.A. I can't stand this waiting around.

MARIE (throwing down cards):
> Let me go along, Roy, please. I sure would like to take in a movie. Please, Roy.

ROY:
> All right . . . Get your hat . . . Hurry up.

MARIE:
> I won't be a second.

She runs out of the cabin.

ROY (puts on his hat):
> We'll be back tomorrow in plenty of time in case Mendoza calls . . . if he ever calls.

He goes out.

129.   EXT. CABIN   MED. SHOT   CAR
Roy comes out of the cabin, gets in the car, steps on the starter. Marie appears immediately carrying a coat. She gets in beside Roy. Red and Babe have come out and are standing on the steps.

ROY:
You guys keep your noses clean.

BABE:
Sure we will, Roy.

130.   MED. CLOSE SHOT   PARD
sitting on the steps of the cabin. His ears are down and he wears a forlorn expression. OVER SCENE the SOUND of the gears.

131.   MED. SHOT   THE BUICK
as Roy turns the car onto the road. Pard runs into scene barking sharply, follows the car. PAN with Pard as he runs in the dust set up by the wheels. He overtakes the car. It slows down, stops.

132.   CLOSE SHOT   PARD   ON THE ROAD
beside the running board of the car.

ROY'S VOICE (OVER SCENE):
Go back, Pard. Go back.

Pard sits down in the road.

CAMERA MOVES UP TO:

133.   INT. CAR   CLOSE SHOT   MARIE AND ROY

MARIE:
Let's take him along, Roy. It'll be nice.

ROY (scratching his head):
I don't know. I got to leave him sometime. He might just as well get used to it.

MARIE:
Yeah . . . you've got to leave him sometime . . . so let's take him now.

Roy looks at her, frowns quizzically.

CAMERA PULLS BACK TO:

134.   MED. CLOSE SHOT
as Roy opens the car door.

ROY:
> Come on, Pard.

The little dog gives a yelp of joy and jumps in. Marie hugs him. The car begins to move.

135.   INT. CAR   CLOSE SHOT   ROY AND MARIE

ROY:
> You want to go to a movie when we get to L.A.?

MARIE:
> I don't care. I just came for the ride.

ROY:
> I guess I'll have to take Pard with me, if you're going to a movie.

MARIE:
> Where are you going?

ROY (hesitating):
> I'm going to see some people . . . friends of mine.

MARIE:
> What racket are they in?

ROY (laughs):
> They're not in any racket. Pa's just a farmer from Ohio . . . lost his farm. There's him and Ma and their granddaughter.

MARIE:
> Granddaughter, huh?

ROY:
> Yeah. Her name's Velma. She just had an operation for her foot . . . she was lame. Mighty pretty girl.

MARIE:
> Is she?

ROY:

You bet . . . and decent.

Marie glances at Roy. He is completely unaware of the cruelty in his words. Marie turns her face away from him. She is hurt and sad.

DISSOLVE TO:

136. INT. PARLOR   BAUGHMAN HOME   MED. SHOT
Pa is nodding in a chair, holding the corner of a news-paper, pages of which have slipped down from his knees onto the floor. The SOUND of Velma's and Ma's voices from the other room, the words indistinguishable. The SOUND of a car door slamming outside and steps on the walk. There is a knock on the door. Pa wakes up with a jerk. The knock is repeated. He pushes up out of the chair, goes to the door, opens it. It is Roy.

ROY:

Hello, Pa.

PA (delightedly):

Roy, I'll be doggoned. Say, where you been?

ROY (ignoring the question):

How's Velma?

Roy enters the room, Pard at his heels.

PA:

You won't know her.

ROY:

You mean she's walking around?

PA:

She's still in bed but the doctor says in a few more days she can dance or do anything, and nobody will ever know she was crippled.

ROY:

Boy, that's great!

The old man bends over, snaps his fingers at Pard.

PA:
> Hi, boy . . . ! Hi, boy!

Pard goes to Pa, who pats him.

PA:
> Mighty cute little feller.

Ma enters the room, sees Roy.

MA (putting her arms around him):
> Roy! It's about time! (She gives him a kiss on the cheek.)

PA:
> You cut that out, Ma. Roy's a darned nice-looking feller and I'm jealous! (Laughs loudly.)

MA:
> Come on in and see Velma.

She takes Roy by the hand and leads him out of the room.

137.   INT. VELMA'S BEDROOM   CLOSE SHOT   VELMA   IN BED
sitting up with pillows at her back. She is fully dressed but has a comforter drawn over her knees. She is reading a letter.

MA'S VOICE (OVER SCENE):
> Mabel's husband's at work and Mabel's uptown gadding around so we got her all to ourselves today, Roy.

Velma quickly buries the letter in a magazine.

138.   MED. SHOT   VELMA'S BEDROOM
as Roy enters followed by Pa and Ma.

ROY (grinning):
> I hear you're all right.

Velma holds out her hands toward him in an awkward way.

MA (nudging Roy):
> She wants to kiss you.

VELMA:
> Oh, Ma!

Roy goes to the bedside, bends down. Velma puts her arms up and presses a little kiss against his cheek.

VELMA:
> We were wondering what happened to you, Roy.

ROY (embarrassed):
> I been pretty busy.

VELMA (seeing Pard):
> Oh! What a cute little dog!

She puts her hands out to him timidly.

PA:
> Don't be afraid of him, honey. He won't bite.

ROY:
> No . . . he won't bite.

VELMA:
> I'm kind of scared of dogs.

Pard retires to a corner. Pa pulls up a chair and Roy sits down beside the bed.

ROY:
> Did it hurt much when they fixed your foot?

VELMA:
> It didn't hurt at all. I didn't even know it.

MA (to Pard):
> I bet he'd like a drink of water. What's his name, Roy?

ROY:
> Pard.

MA:
> Come on, Pard.

She signals with her head to Pa to come, too. Pard follows them out of the room.

139. CLOSE SHOT ROY AND VELMA
There is an embarrassed silence which lasts several moments. Roy looks at the cover of the magazine. There is a picture of Bette Davis on the cover.

VELMA:
> Do you ever read magazines like this, Roy?

ROY:
> Nope . . . not me.

VELMA:
> What do you read?

ROY (embarrassed laugh):
> The sports page.

VELMA:
> Don't you ever read books?

ROY:
> Well, I read a few books when I had nothing else to do.[10]

VELMA:
> I guess you'd rather do things yourself than read about other people doing things. I'll be more that way now . . . I read an awful lot back home. We had a nice library in Barrowville.

ROY (frowning):
> You'll dance and run around now—and that's what you ought to be doing.

VELMA:
> We'll never get through thanking you, Roy. It was wonderful of you.

ROY (after a pause):

> I got a big business deal coming up, Velma. I figure if it goes through the way it ought to, I can retire for life.

VELMA (lightly):

> Oh, that's fine, Roy. Did you tell Pa? He'll be tickled to hear it.

ROY:

> Look, Velma, did you ever think you'd like to go around the world?

VELMA:

> Around the world? Oh, I don't know if I'd like that. It's so far. It would take so long to get back.

ROY:

> I was figuring if this deal goes through, I'd like to go around the world and I was just . . . (Hesitating, glancing up.) You see what I mean, Velma?

VELMA (in a little voice):

> Yes . . . I see.

ROY:

> Well . . . I was just thinking . . . If you wouldn't want to go around the world, what would you like to do? I'd . . . I'd . . . sure like to marry you, Velma. I'm not so old and I'm going to have plenty of money.

He keeps his eyes averted for moment, then he looks at her. She smiles uncertainly. It is a weak smile.

VELMA:

> I don't know . . . (She plucks at the comforter.) You sure been wonderful to us and Pa says there's no better man than you, but, Roy . . .

Her voice trails off. She stares steadily at the comforter.

140.   CLOSE-UP   VELMA
as tears gather and glisten on her long eyelashes.

ROY'S VOICE (his voice husky):
>You got somebody back home, I guess.

VELMA:
>Yes, in a way I have. He's . . .

She hides her face in the comforter and sobs.

141.   CLOSE SHOT   THE TWO

ROY:
>He figuring on coming out here to marry you?

VELMA:
>I don't know. I may go back there. I ought to be hearing from him any day now. He writes a couple of times a week.

ROY:
>Did you tell him your foot was cured?

VELMA:
>I had to . . . I mean . . . I thought . . . Oh, Roy, maybe we shouldn't have let you do what you did.

ROY:
>Are you really crazy about him, Velma?

Velma doesn't answer, nor will she meet Roy's gaze. Suddenly she hides her face in the comforter. Then she nods her head vigorously three times. Roy pushes back his chair, gets up.

ROY (haltingly):
>Well, I guess that lets me out.

VELMA (showing her face):
>We can still be friends though, can't we, Roy?

Roy can only nod. He edges toward the door.

VELMA:
>When will we see you again?

ROY:
> I don't know.

VELMA:
> I'll be walking in a few days.

Pa comes in with Pard.

VELMA:
> Roy, you simply must come back to see me walk.

Pa looks from Roy to Velma, then back to Roy.

PA (uncertainly):
> Why . . . of course, he will.

ROY:
> Yeah . . . sure . . . I'll come back to see Velma walk.

Pard follows Roy out of the room. Pa runs after. OVER SCENE the SOUND of Pa's voice and the front door closing. Velma starts crying again. Pa comes back into the room.

PA:
> Why, pet, what's wrong?

VELMA:
> He wants me to marry him, Pa, and I said I wouldn't on account of Lon.

PA (crestfallen):
> Oh.

VELMA (tearfully):
> I been through so much lately . . . the hospital and everything and then I don't know what Lon's going to do and . . . [11]

PA (patting her shoulder):
> There . . . There . . .

DISSOLVE TO:

142.   INT. CAR   CLOSE SHOT   NIGHT
        ROY AND MARIE   (PROCESS)
        They are heading back for the camp. Marie is holding
        Pard in her lap, and he is leaning out the window of the
        car, his nose to the wind.

        MARIE:
            Pard's sure enjoying the ride. (Looking at Roy, who
            seems older.) What's the matter, Roy?

        ROY (angrily):
            Nothing. What makes you think anything's the
            matter?

        MARIE:
            You ain't said ten words since we left L.A. (She puts
            her hand on his knee.) I think I know . . .

        ROY (after a silence):
            It looks like you and me.

        Marie slides down in the seat, lets her head rest on Roy's
        shoulder. His eyes go back to the road.

        ROY:
            Yeah . . .

                                                    FADE OUT
        FADE IN
143.   MED. LONG SHOT   SHAW'S CAMP
        Algernon makes tracks up the road past CAMERA and to-
        ward the cabins. He wears a mackinaw.

144.   EXT. ROY'S CABIN
        as Algernon comes into the scene. Smoke is coming out
        of the chimney. Algernon knocks at the door. It is opened
        by Marie.

145.   INT. ROY'S CABIN
        SHOOTING past Roy in foreground.

        ALGERNON:
            Mornin'. Man at Ballard phoned in a telegram for

Mr. Collins. How you all, people? Ain't it cold though? Hello there, Pard, you lucky dog, you.

Roy rises. Marie hands him the message. He opens it. Algernon leaves, and Marie shuts the door.

146.   INSERT MESSAGE
in Roy's hand. It reads:
MARIPOSE THIRD RACE BEST BET.[12]
M.

147.   CLOSE SHOT ROY

ROY:
It's from Mendoza . . . Tonight's the big night.
                                    DISSOLVE TO:

148.   INT. RED AND BABE'S CABIN

MED. SHOT ROY, RED, BABE, AND MARIE
Red and Babe are stowing the hammers and other articles of equipment into a big sack. Roy checks each item as it goes into the sack and scratches it off a list.

BABE:
Here's the three hammers. Do you think we'll need the sledge, Roy?

ROY:
I dunno. I never busted into no safety-deposit boxes before.

BABE:
I still don't see why Mendoza can't open the boxes.

ROY:
It would be a tip-off that it was an inside job. They'd pinch Mendoza and he'd sing—or I don't know nothin' about guys.

MARIE:
What about Pard?

ROY (scowls, then after a pause):
Take Pard over to Algernon. Tell him to keep that dog locked up till we get away. Give him five bucks.

MARIE:
Roy, I was thinkin' . . . Why not take Pard along?

RED (slapping his leg):
Imagine taking a dog on a caper! That's rich—that is!

Roy glares at Red. He sobers instantly.

MARIE:
I'd watch after him, Roy.

ROY (angrily):
Do like I told you!

She picks up Pard, exits with him in her arms.

ROY (runs his finger down the list):
I guess that's everything . . . Now look, fellows, in a few minutes we're going for the coconuts. Let's get things straight. When we get into the hotel, don't even look up no matter what happens. That's my job. Nobody's going to bother you and I mean nobody. Any questions?

Red and Babe both shake their heads.

ROY:
This caper's a cinch. Marie and I take the jewelry in the shoe box and head for L.A. You take the dough and come back up here. That way we won't all be ganging up together. When you get word from me, bring the dough to L.A.

They both nod.

ROY:
Well, I guess we're all set.

RED:

    I'm glad Marie's coming . . . She's all right—got more nerve than most guys.

ROY:

    We'll make up her share between us. That's fair, ain't it?

BABE:

    Yeah.

RED:

    You bet. It's worth it to have somebody looking after the car.

They start to carry the sack and suitcase out on the porch.

149.   EXT. PORCH OF CABIN
as they load sack and suitcase into cars.

RED (continuing):

    I'll never forget what happened to a guy I know—Petty Garrison . . . Small-timer he was. He and another hood waltzed in to heist a grocery store. They left the heap out in front with the engine runnin'. When they came bustin' out a coupla jumps ahead of a shotgun blast, some so-and-so had stolen it. They ducked down an alley and run right into a big copper. Brother, what a mess!

BABE:

    You sure can think up the prettiest stories to tell!

RED:

    Aw, they was just small-timers—not like us.

BABE:

    We wasn't so big till this one . . . I don't feel big.

RED:

    Roy feels big. That's what counts.

Marie comes in.

MARIE:
> Algernon's got Pard locked in his cabin. Funny—
> Pard knows there's something up. He keeps scratch-
> ing at the door.

ROY (bursting out):
> That little mutt's a plain nuisance!

OVER SCENE the SOUND of barking, following by sharp,
insistent yelps. Marie glances at Roy, who turns away.

ROY:
> Get going, you guys.

OVER SCENE a long howl, a high-pitched unearthly wail
which dies away slowly.

MARIE:
> That's Pard. I told you he knew.

ROY:
> Shut up and get in the car. (To Red and Babe.) Well,
> what are you standing there for? I told you to get
> going.

RED:
> Okay, Roy.

OVER SCENE another long howl.

BABE:
> I wish that dog'd stop howling. I don't like it. It gives
> me the creeps.

They drive off.

150.   INT. CAR   CLOSE SHOT   MOONLIGHT
ROY AND MARIE   (PROCESS)
as they drive past the general store and out onto the dark
highway. Marie turns in her seat to take a last look at the
lake. She gives a gasp and then begins to laugh a little
hysterically.

ROY:
> What's wrong with you?

MARIE:
> It's Pard—he got loose—here he comes.

151.   LONG SHOT   ROAD   PARD
running down the middle of the road toward the car.

152.   INT. CAR   ROY AND MARIE
Roy steps on the gas.

ROY:
> He can't follow us far at night.

MARIE:
> Roy, you can't . . .

ROY:
> Who says I can't?

There's a short silence. Then Roy jams on the brakes, pulls over to the side of the road.

ROY:
> What I ought to do is put a bullet in his head. Ain't I got enough trouble without a fool dog?

153.   EXT. CAR   PARKED ON SIDE OF ROAD
Pard comes up panting, jumps on the running board, tries to leap in the car. He misses his footing and rolls his back in the dust.

ROY'S VOICE (OVER SCENE):
> Pard!

The little dog sits up and barks sharply. Marie opens the door on her side, and Pard is around the car like a shot and in between them on the seat.

154.   INT. CAR   ROY AND MARIE   NIGHT
with Pard sitting between them on the seat.

MARIE:
> Poor little devil! Got no home . . . got nobody.

ROY (starting up again):
> Of all the fourteen-carat saps! Starting out on a caper with a woman and a dog! If he spoils this job, I'll . . .

MARIE:
> Oh, you're full of talk! I think you're glad.

There is a long silence. Then Roy reaches over and pats Pard. Marie's face is suddenly all tenderness. She puts her arm around him and kisses him on the cheek. He starts the car again. They drive for some time in silence. At last they come out on Broken Creek Summit.

ROY:
> Some country! I bet it looks like this on the moon.

155. LONG SHOT   BROKEN CREEK SUMMIT
The car, a black speck, is moving across the plateau. CAMERA PANS up the granite side of the mountain, up and up to its summit.

DISSOLVE TO:

156. EXT. TROPICO INN   SIDE ROAD
as the two cars—one driven by Roy and the other by Red—pull into scene and come to a halt. There is just enough light to see the shadowy figures as they emerge from the cars. Marie remains in the first car.

ROY (whispering to Red and Babe):
> You guys know just what to do. Use your heads. (To Marie.) Keep your eyes open, kid.

DISSOLVE TO:

157. INT. DIMLY LIT HOTEL LOBBY   MED. LONG SHOT
A log fire is burning, casting flickering reflections on the white walls. Mendoza is leaning against the desk looking at a magazine. A bellboy is yawning on his bench. OVER

SCENE the SOUND of the door opening. The bellboy looks up, starts to yawn again, then his jaws clamp shut and he springs up.

BELLBOY (squeals):
M . . . Mendoza!

158.   ANOTHER ANGLE   OF LOBBY
from behind desk, Mendoza in foreground as Roy, Red, and Babe enter and start across the lobby. Roy carries his .45.

ROY (to bellboy):
Shut up.

The bellboy drops back onto his bench.

ROY:
One move out of you, son, and I'll fill your pants full of lead.

BELLBOY (frightened stiff):
Yes, sir . . . don't you worry about me, sir . . .

Red and Babe come around behind the desk.

RED (points to safe; to Mendoza in a harsh voice for bellboy's benefit):
Open it quick before I let air through you.

159.   CLOSE SHOT   SAFE
as Mendoza pushes the safe door. Packages of bills are in neat stacks on the floor. Red and Babe stuff their pockets full. Babe takes the shoe box out of the sack, puts it on the floor behind the desk. Then they get out their ball peen hammers and start banging away at the safe-deposit boxes. The racket is deafening.

160.   CLOSE SHOT   ROY
his back to the desk, running his eyes over the three sides of the lobby which face the verandah. In the background

behind the desk, Red and Babe are swinging away at the boxes. Mendoza stands at an angle to the desk with his hands in the air. Roy shouts above the noise:

ROY:
How's it going?

RED (shouting back):
Having a little trouble with the boxes.

161.   CLOSE SHOT   RED
as he smashes one of the boxes, reaches inside, and takes out a handful of jewelry.

RED:
Plenty of rocks! Boy!

He puts the jewelry into the shoe box. PAN CAMERA to Babe as he breaks open a box, puts in his hand, takes out jewelry. PAN CAMERA around past Mendoza to Roy, who stands as before, watching the windows.

ROY:
How are you doing?

RED'S VOICE (OVER SCENE):
Got a few more. Boy, is this a haul!

Roy stiffens. There is a shadow on the verandah. Through the window he sees a man and woman coming toward the lobby. The man bangs back the big door.

162.   CLOSE SHOT   DOOR
There is a momentary lull in the hammering as the man and woman enter. The woman is bundled up in a beautiful white wrap. They are both tight.

WOMAN:
Oh, I'm frozen! Look at the fire, Bob. Doesn't that look . . .

CAMERA PANS them as they walk across the lobby to the
fire. Roy watches from background. Now the hammering
breaks out again louder than ever.

MAN:
Nice time of night to build a house.

They stand swaying. Then the woman sees Roy's gun.

WOMAN (screaming):
Bob, look!

The man blinks, steps forward, halts.

163.   REVERSE ANGLE   ROY IN FOREGROUND
his back to CAMERA.

RED'S VOICE (OVER SCENE):
A couple more and we got it.

WOMAN (screams):
My rings, Bob. You've got to stop them . . . My rings!

MAN (to Roy):
Look, my friend, you can't do this. I mean, you can't
. . . you . . .

ROY:
Go sit by the fire, both of you, and you won't get
hurt.

The woman gives a low scream. Her legs begin to buckle.

ROY:
Take care of her, you fool![13]

The man catches the woman just as she is about to sink to
the floor.

MAN:
Don't shoot. Give me time. I'll get her over to the fire.
Take it easy, I'll get her . . .

ROY:
> Stay where you are. Lie down and stay down. (The
> man obeys.) That's perfect. Now, be quiet.

The man and woman lie quietly. CAMERA MOVES UP on
Roy, who is watching.

164. CLOSE-UP MENDOZA
The strain is beginning to tell on him. His forehead is
wet and his jaw muscles are working.

165. CLOSE SHOT MAN AND WOMAN ON FLOOR
MAN (in a low distracted tone):
> Darling, speak to me . . . say something . . . wake
> up . . . Oh, darling! (He looks up.) I'm scared . . . I
> don't know . . .

166. REVERSE ANGLE MED. CLOSE SHOT ROY
his back to CAMERA.

ROY:
> You lie still and don't give me no trouble. We'll be
> through here shortly.

MAN:
> You'll never get away with this.

ROY:
> Okay.

RED'S VOICE (OVER SCENE):
> With you in a minute.

167.–168. CLOSE-UP SHOE BOX
Babe's hand comes into the picture, drops jewelry into
the box.

169. EXT. HOTEL CLOSE SHOT MARIE IN CAR
Pard, in her lap, is listening with cocked head to the
racket of the hammers. OVER SCENE comes another SOUND,

the sound of feet on gravel. Marie starts, looks around. CAMERA PULLS BACK and in the background a man in a big western hat and puttees is walking rapidly toward the hotel verandah. Marie touches the horn.

170.   FULL SHOT   LOBBY
as OVER SCENE the SOUND of the horn, followed by barking. The hammering ceases. Roy puts his back against the desk. The door opens and the tall man enters. He wears a Sam Brown belt, a leather holster swings at his hip.

MENDOZA (weakly):
Watchman.

ROY (without turning):
Shut up.

The watchman walks straight into the lobby unbuttoning his holster. He has a hard, leathery face and close-clipped moustache. He peers at Roy as if he couldn't see very well. Roy swings his gun on him.

ROY:
Heist 'em, buddy.

The watchman slowly begins to raise his hands.

MENDOZA:
He ain't got his glasses.

WATCHMAN:
No, Mendoza, I ain't. I busted them this afternoon. What's going on here?

ROY:
Never mind . . . Just keep your trap shut.

BABE (calling):
Let's get goin' . . . Come on, quick. There may be more of 'em.

ROY:
Keep your shirts on. It's nothing.

The woman on the floor sits up and screams piercingly. Roy glances momentarily in her direction. A gun roars in the stillness and a bullet clips a big splinter off the desk just to the left of Roy's ear. Roy fires at the watchman. Mendoza, Babe, and Red all fall down behind the desk. The watchman gives a low cry of surprise and pain, falls to the floor with a groan. His head sinks and he lies on his side, groaning.

ROY:
> Sorry, brother, but I guess you ain't killed. I shot low enough.

The woman screams again, a wild, hair-raising scream as if she were being tortured. Roy turns.

ROY:
> Come on, guys, let's get going!

He starts across the lobby. Red hurries over to him, puts the shoe box under his left arm. Babe rushes up out of breath, followed by Mendoza, who looks like something dead and dug up.

ROY (to Mendoza):
> Where are you going?

MENDOZA:
> I'm going with you. I'm all shot. I couldn't face the police now.

ROY:
> Okay. Come on.

The woman is still screaming. They cross the lobby quickly and go out.

171.   EXT. HOTEL   TRUCKING SHOT
as Roy, Babe, Red, and Mendoza go quickly over the lawn. Mendoza is blubbering.

MENDOZA:
> I never thought we'd have to shoot anybody.

ROY:
> He won't croak. I shot low . . .

MENDOZA (stops):
> I'm going to faint, I think. Help me. I guess I better go back. I don't know if . . .

Roy kicks him and he straightens up with a jerk.

ROY:
> Snap out of it, Mendoza. We got trouble enough without you blowing your top.

OVER SCENE the muffled SOUND of a police siren.

BABE:
> There's the rumble.

172.   MED. SHOT   THE CARS

MARIE (calls):
> Roy!

They go up to the car.

RED:
> You're a sweetheart, Marie. All right, Babe. Let's go places and fast. Come on, Mendoza, hop in.

The three men get in the car, the motor roars, and the car moves off.

MARIE:
> Come on, Roy. Hurry! The siren's getting nearer.

ROY:
> Okay. Here we go! Where's Pard?

MARIE:
> He's in the rumble seat. I was afraid he'd get lost

when we started to blow. When I saw that copper
crossing the plaza, I knew you'd come running.

ROY:

I had to take care of him.

MARIE:

Yeah . . . I heard the shots.

The gears grind. The car moves away.

173. INT. CAR   CLOSE SHOT   NIGHT
ROY AND MARIE   (PROCESS)

ROY:

Babe's crazy driving without lights.

They are driving very fast. The SOUND of the siren comes
nearer and nearer.

ROY:

He better switch on them lights. What's he doing?
He's turning off.

174. LONG SHOT   FORK IN ROAD
Babe's car is turning to the left, the tires shrieking.

175. INT. CAR   ROY AND MARIE
Roy stops his car, stares up the road Babe has taken.

ROY:

He's taking the wrong road.

MARIE:

What are you gonna do?

ROY:

Going after them.

MARIE:

Don't worry about him, worry about us.

OVER SCENE a loud CRASH of a collision, followed by a shattering, jolting, ripping series of SOUNDS.

MARIE:
> They've had an accident. Oh, Roy!

ROY:
> Now they done it. Lost their heads! Small-timers for small jobs! This was too big.

The siren gets louder and louder.

MARIE:
> Their car's on fire.

176. LONG SHOT   ROAD
Several hundred feet up the road to the left there is a red glow, then flames spring up.

177. INT. CAR   ROY AND MARIE

ROY (starts up again, steps on the accelerator):
> Up in smoke. Well, it's a break for us anyway. Them coppers will go to the fire.

They drive along for several moments in silence.

ROY:
> I done my share. That's all a guy can do.

MARIE:
> Roy?

ROY:
> Yeah?

MARIE (quietly):
> I'm about ready to pass out . . . no fooling . . .

She slides sideways and falls against him with a groan. Roy manages to get her head on his shoulder without slackening speed.

DISSOLVE TO:

178. LONG SHOT   CAR
Roy is driving fast, as before.

DISSOLVE TO:

179. INT. CAR   ROY AND MARIE
Marie moans, stirs, opens her eyes, looks around in bewilderment, then remembers.

MARIE:
I fainted, I guess.

ROY:
You sure did. (Slows down, applies brakes.) I'm going to get Pard out of the rumble seat. Guys that stick up places don't carry dogs around with them. Get me?

He pulls over to the side of the road and stops.[14]

180. EXT. CAR   MED. CLOSE SHOT
Roy opens the rumble seat, lifts Pard out, puts him down. CAMERA PANS with the little dog as he runs to a fence post, smells.

181. EXT. CAR   CLOSE SHOT   MARIE
Roy comes into scene.

ROY:
You feel all right?

MARIE:
Kind of wobbly.

OVER SCENE a rooster crows.

MARIE:
What about Babe and Red?

ROY (shrugging):
If they didn't kick off, the coppers have 'em.

MARIE:
Think they'll talk?

ROY:

    Nope . . . but Mendoza will.

MARIE:

    You're in a spot, ain't you?

ROY:

    If I am, it ain't worryin' me any—and I'm not bragging. I'm just used to jams, that's all. Okay, Pard.

He holds the door open and Pard jumps in the front seat. Roy gets in.

182.   INT. CAR   ROY AND MARIE

as Roy drives on.

ROY:

    We'll be in soon. Then I'll turn the glass over to Mac and he'll hand me a big roll. We got a fortune in this car, Marie.

MARIE:

    I'll feel better when we're rid of it.

ROY:

    You got quite a piece of dough coming, and I'm gonna see that you get it right away because I'll be blowing pretty soon. Going back east, I guess.

MARIE:

    I'm going with you.

ROY:

    Don't be a sap. They don't want you. If you run around with me, you'll never be in anything but trouble.

MARIE (looks at him):

    Are you trying to ditch me on account of that Little Eva from the corn belt?

ROY:

Nope . . . not on account of her. It's—well, it's just too tough a life. No woman can take it.

MARIE:

I bet I can do a better job of it than any woman you ever met before.

ROY:

That's no lie.

MARIE:

I'm sticking with you, Roy. (Puts her arm through Roy's, sits up close.) Don't think you're ever gonna check me so easy. I never been so happy in my life. I'm a different girl. I feel clean.

Their faces are beginning to get light. Dawn is breaking.

ROY (laughs):

Well, we'll see. If the going gets too tough, I may have to park you for a while.

MARIE:

I'm glad you said "for a while" . . . that makes me feel good. If I really get in your way, you can park me. Is it a deal?

ROY:

It's a deal . . . It's getting daylight. Funny—I still like to see that sun come up.

DISSOLVE TO:

183.   EXT. BERLAND ARMS APARTMENTS

Roy's car pulls up in front. He gets out with the shoe box under his arm. Marie has to keep Pard from jumping out after him.

ROY:

I won't be long.

He goes up the steps.

184.   INT. HALLWAY OUTSIDE BIG MAC'S APARTMENT   ROY comes quickly down the hall, stops, raises his hand to press the buzzer on Big Mac's door, hesitates, opens his coat, takes the automatic out of the waistband of his trousers, puts it in his side pocket, then he touches the buzzer. The door is immediately opened. Roy takes a step backward. Kranmer stands there grinning at him.

KRANMER:
Hello, Earle.

Roy brushes past him.

185.   INT. LIVING ROOM   BIG MAC'S APARTMENT

ROY:
What are you doing here?

KRANMER:
Big Mac sent for me. I flew out a couple of days ago . . . Awful sick man, Big Mac is . . . collapsed last night. He's asleep.

He picks up a newspaper, holds it up so Roy can see the headlines.

INSERT   NEWSPAPER HEADLINE[15]
It reads:
TROPICO STUNNED BY HALF MILLION
DOLLAR ROBBERY
BACK TO SCENE:
Roy takes the paper, reads down the column.

KRANMER:
Tough about the two guys.

ROY (glancing up):
It was their own fault.

KRANMER:
Well, their troubles are over.

ROY (matter-of-fact):
Both got it, huh?

KRANMER:

Yeah . . . Mendoza broke his collarbone, got knocked cold but he'll be all right. (Laughs.) The police think he was kidnapped and they ain't identified Red and Babe yet . . . But, Earle, you really knicked 'em. Let's go show the stuff to Big Mac. It may pep him up. You got it there in that shoe box?

ROY:

Yeah, and it sure is heavy.

Kranmer pushes open the door, leads the way in.

186.   INT. BEDROOM   MED. CLOSE SHOT   ON BED
as Roy and Kranmer come to the bedside. Big Mac is lying on his side, his face turned to the wall. Roy opens the shoe box, begins to put some jewels out on Big Mac's night table. Kranmer shakes Mac gently.

KRANMER:

Wake up, boss. Earle's here. He clipped 'em for half a million.

ROY:

Yeah . . . I sure come through for you, Mac. You didn't spring me for nothin'.

KRANMER:

Mac, wake up. Wake up . . . Earle's here.

There is a moment's silence, then Kranmer glances up blankly at Earle.

KRANMER:

This guy's dead.

ROY:

He's what?

KRANMER:
> He's dead. (He touches Big Mac's hand.) Yep . . .
> cold as a mackerel. Kicked off in his sleep, I guess.

Roy stands stunned, rubbing his chin.

KRANMER:
> This is sure a mess.

Roy begins to gather up the jewelry, puts it back in the
shoe box. Kranmer watches him with a furtive look on
his face.

KRANMER:
> What are you going to do with that stuff?

ROY:
> Mac told me just what to do in case something like
> this come up. I guess he had a feeling he'd never
> make it.

KRANMER (excitedly):
> Earle, don't be a sap! Mac's dead—and we're rich! I
> can get a fence to handle the stuff. Don't you get it?
> We're rich!

ROY:
> Listen, chiseler. I'm still working for Mac, and so are
> you. I got instructions and I'm going to follow 'em.

KRANMER (wildly):
> Use your head, man! This is the biggest break you'll
> ever get in your life!

ROY (softly):
> You heard me.

KRANMER (after a pause; craftily):
> Okay, Earle, maybe you're right. Sorry I talked out of
> turn.

He goes into the living room. Roy sits down on the bedside, takes out the envelope Big Mac gave him, tears it

open, studies the letter, then picks up the telephone and dials a number.

ROY (after a moment):
Is this Pico 7719 . . . ? That you, E.D. . . . ? This is R. . . .

An indistinct voice in the receiver.

ROY (into phone):
M.'s dead. He said in the letter to call you. You're supposed to do the handling. (SOUND of the voice.) Nope . . . he just kicked off . . . his heart . . . (SOUND of voice again.)

The gold fountain pen is on the night table. Roy picks it up, writes down an address on the margin of the racing form.
                                    CAMERA PULLS BACK SLOWLY TO:

187.   FULL SHOT   BEDROOM
Kranmer stands in the door, a big automatic in his right hand, his face twitching.

ROY (into phone):
Okay . . . Thanks.

Roy hangs up, turns around, sees Kranmer and the muzzle of the automatic.

KRANMER:
Hand over that box, Earle. Give me any trouble and I'll fill you full of lead. I'd be reinstated and get a medal besides.

ROY (slowly; shaking his head):
A copper's always a copper. (He rises.) Well, this stuff's pretty hot at that. (Picks up the box with his left hand and extends it to Kranmer.) You're welcome to it.

188.   MED. SHOT   ROY   KRANMER IN FOREGROUND
back to CAMERA. Roy steps forward holding out the box.

He is smiling but his eyes look merciless and hard as flint. He slides his right hand into his coat pocket. Kranmer takes half a step backward.

KRANMER:
Don't . . . .

Then Kranmer fires. Simultaneously, Roy fires through his coat pocket. Kranmer reels, clutches at the door jamb, then slides slowly down out of the picture. Roy feels his own left side, then looks at his fingers. They are bloody. Swearing under his breath, he goes back to the telephone, dials a number.[16]

ROY (calmly into phone):
Mr. Parker, please . . . (After a few minutes.) Hello, Doc, this is Roy . . . Yeah . . . Can I see you right away?

189.   INT. HALLWAY   MED. LONG SHOT
Two doors are open, and a blonde and a brunette are talking across the hall.

BLONDE:
It certainly sounded like shooting.

BRUNETTE:
Yeah. And right close, like it was in one of the apartments.

The door to Big Mac's apartment opens and Roy appears, comes toward CAMERA.

BRUNETTE (to Roy):
Did you hear shooting?

Roy holds his hat so that it covers his left side.

ROY:
Why, no ma'am, I didn't.

BLONDE:
> I thought I did. It sounded close but I got the window up so maybe it was outside.

ROY:
> Might have been a truck. Personally, I didn't hear a thing.

He comes on down the hall toward the stairs.

190. EXT. APARTMENT BUILDING   CLOSE SHOT   MARIE
pacing up and down beside the car. Her face looks grayish. When Roy comes out of the apartment house, she groans with relief.

MARIE:
> What happened? I was getting ready to go look for you.

ROY:
> Get in. You got to drive.

MARIE:
> What's wrong, honey?

ROY:
> I got a slug in me, I think.

He gets into the car. Marie runs around the car, gets into the driver's seat. She starts up the car.

191. INT. CAR   ROY AND MARIE

ROY:
> Go to Vermont and turn right.

Marie glances at him, then puts the car into gear. Pard whimpers uneasily.

ROY:
> He smells blood.

> > > > DISSOLVE TO:

192.   INT. NU-HEALTH INSTITUTE   DOC'S OFFICE
Roy is lying face down on a table smoking a cigarette
while Doc works on him.

DOC:

>   You're lucky, Roy. A little to the left and you'da had
>   a shattered pelvis.

ROY (wincing):

>   Yeah . . . (Sitting up.) That stuff sure burns, Doc.

DOC:

>   Here, take this bottle with you and these extra dress-
>   ings. Change it every day. (Helping him with his
>   shirt.) Did you really crack 'em for five hundred G's,
>   Roy?

ROY:

>   Can't tell yet, Doc. They always kick up the price
>   after a heist, but we got lots of rocks . . . By the way,
>   you're gonna have to trust me on the dough angle. I
>   ain't got but fifty-sixty dollars.

DOC:

>   Didn't get your end yet, eh? All right, Roy, but I fig-
>   ure this is going to cost five hundred dollars when
>   you do get it. I'm taking an awful chance.

ROY:

>   Five hundred is okay by me. When I need help, I
>   need help bad, and I'm willing to pay for it.

DOC:

>   Take a tip from old Doc, Roy, and blow . . . blow
>   fast.

ROY:

>   I'm blowing.

DOC:

>   What about little Velma?[17]

ROY (embarrassed):
>I don't know, Doc. That was just one of them things
>. . . I got a dame that can stand the gaff and I'm tak-
>ing her with me.

DOC:
>Yeah . . . ? Well, you better get going, Roy. If you
>get taken up here, I'll be sunk. They'd start looking
>me up and I'd be keeping you company in San
>Quentin. I'm sixty years old. A short jolt would fin-
>ish me.

ROY:
>So long, Doc . . . Thanks.

DOC:
>Good luck, Roy.

They shake hands. Roy goes. Doc crosses to the window, looks out.

193. MED. SHOT STREET THROUGH WINDOW
SHOOTING over Doc's shoulder. Marie is standing beside the car while Pard runs about.

DOC (ejaculates):
>Well, I'll be . . . a woman and a dog!

After a moment Roy appears. Doc sees the man, the woman, and the dog get into the car. The car moves off.

DOC (shakes his head):
>Just a big farmer . . .

194. INT. CAR MARIE AND ROY (PROCESS)
Marie is driving.

ROY:
>Make a right turn here.

MARIE (surprised):
>What about getting rid of the stuff! Ain't we going
>to Santa Monica?

ROY:

> There's something I've got to do first. It ain't much out of the way.

MARIE:

> Little Velma, huh?

ROY:

> I promised Pa I'd come and see her walk.

MARIE:

> Fine time you picked to go calling. If we get knocked over, it'll be your fault. (Suddenly.) Can I go in with you?

ROY (hesitatingly):
> Well . . . sure . . . if you want to . . .

195. INT. BAUGHMAN LIVING ROOM
CLOSE SHOT   VELMA'S FEET AND HER PARTNER'S
Velma is wearing high-heeled shoes.

> CAMERA PULLS BACK TO:

196. CLOSE SHOT   VELMA AND LON PREISER
as they dance to the radio music of a hot jitterbug band.

> CAMERA PULLS BACK TO:

197. MED. SHOT   GROUP   VELMA, LON, JOE, AND MARGIE
Joe and Margie are drunk. Joe is about Lon's age and is Lon's friend. Margie is a typical tart type. She and Joe are necking on the sofa, and near them is a table with a pitcher of water and two half-empty bottles of Scotch and gin. There is a great change in Velma's appearance, and it is not for the better. She is sober, but Lon has had a couple.

VELMA (dancing with Lon):
> My foot gets stronger all the time, Lon . . . Don't you think I'm dancing better?

LON:
> You're perfect, baby . . . Would you like a little drink?

VELMA (laughing):
> Oh, no, Lon . . . Do you want me to get dizzy again—
> like last night?

LON (laughing):
> You were cute . . . I like you like that.

On the couch, Margie suddenly gives out a shriek of laughter. Velma and Lon keep on dancing but turn in her direction.

MARGIE (to Joe):
> I don't believe it! (Loud laugh; then, to Lon.) Your
> boyfriend is killin' me! (Laughs again.)

JOE (to Margie, dramatically):
> You're so sweet!

VELMA (worried, to Lon):
> You think they'll be all right?

LON:
> Sure . . . Joe's a panic when he's tight.

There is another shriek of laughter from Margie. Pa appears in the doorway, carrying a paper. He is rubbing his eyes and he looks depressed.

PA:
> Look here now. I was never the one to spoil a good
> time. But enough's enough, I say.

The doorbell rings twice.

PA (further annoyed):
> Who's that now? (Starts toward door.)

MARGIE (to Joe):
> I thought you said we were gonna be alone!

Pa opens the door. Roy enters.

PA (enthused):
> Roy! Well, this *is* a surprise!

VELMA (turns radio down, rushes over excitedly):
> Hello, Roy! It's about time you dropped in. Where have you been?

Roy cannot talk. The change in Velma, the entire surroundings stab at his heart.

PA:
> Rest of the family's out for a ride, Roy. They'll be sorry they missed you.

VELMA:
> Oh, excuse me. Roy, this is Mr. Preiser. He's my— he's from back home.

Roy nods coldly.

LON:
> Hello, Roy. (Puts out hand, which Roy is forced to take.) Velma's told me a lot about you. Matter of fact, we had a couple of drinks to you the other night.

ROY (very slowly):
> Did you?

VELMA (sensing tension):
> Roy, you haven't seen me dance yet. My foot is all better now . . . Watch . . . (She turns up radio, starts dancing by herself.)

198.　　EXT. BAUGHMAN HOME　MARIE AND PARD　IN CAR
Marie is looking impatiently at the door of the cottage. Pard, at car door on right, is also looking at cottage door and whining softly. Marie reaches a decision suddenly and opens door at right.

MARIE:
> Go ahead, Pard . . . Get Roy . . . Find Roy, Pard.

The dog leaps gleefully from the seat and makes a beeline for the door of the Baughman cottage. Marie edges from the driver's seat through the same door and follows right after Pard.

199.   INT. BAUGHMAN HOME

as Velma continues to show Roy that she can dance. Joe suddenly gets up as Velma passes him.

JOE:
> Fine party this is! Letting a lady dance by herself! (Grabbing her.) Come on, honey.

He holds Velma very tightly, whirls her around. Halfheartedly and laughingly, she tries to push him away. But he does not release her and they continue to dance. Roy's face becomes brutal. Looking at him, Lon grows nervous.

LON (worried smile):
> It's all right. That's my pal, Joe Bates. He came west with me, and he's having his little fling. (Winks at Roy, as one wise guy to another.) He don't get away from home very often.

Lon's smile fades as Roy merely glances at him. In background, Margie looks up from sofa.

MARGIE (to Joe):
> Hey, Romeo—what am I supposed to do while you're playin' leap frog?

Joe laughs, lets Velma slip from his grasp, sits beside Margie on sofa, his arm around her.

JOE (dramatically):
> You're so sweet.

There is a scratching at the door, followed by a sharp bark. Velma turns the radio down.

PA:
> I declare. What's all this now?

He opens the door. Pard runs in, followed by Marie. Pard sits up in front of Roy, begging.

MARIE:
Pard, you bad dog, you. (To Roy, obviously lying.) He jumped out of the car before I knew what happened. (As Velma approaches.) Hello. You're Velma, aren't you?

VELMA (surprised):
That's right.

MARIE:
I'm Marie Garson—friend of Roy's . . . I feel as though I know you. Roy's told me so many times how sweet and charming you are.

VELMA:
Has he?

LON:
Say, that reminds me. You did a lot for Velma, Roy, and I feel I ought to pay you back. (Reaching for wallet.) It's quite a bit of money, and—

ROY:
Forget it. Think nothing of it.

VELMA:
But I'd like you to take it, Roy. (Puts her arm in Lon's.) After all, Lon and I are getting married very soon—and he can afford it easily . . .

MARIE:
Getting married, eh? Say, that's fine. Isn't it, Roy?

ROY:
Yeah. Yeah, that's swell. (Swallows hard, turns to Pa.) I guess we'll be on our way, Pa. I—I'm goin' east, and I just wanted to say good-by.

PA:
I don't like to see you rush off like this, Roy.

LON (heartily):
Pa's right. You can't go so soon. What do you say we

all have a drink together, Roy—you and your girlie and my little Velma. (Puts his arm around Roy's shoulder.)

ROY (almost trembling):
Get your hand off me.

LON (frightened):
I—I'm sorry. I—

ROY:
I don't like you. I don't like the way you talk. I don't like your friends . . . I don't like to think of Velma bein' married to you.

MARIE (worried; hand on his arm):
Roy—

VELMA:
I think you'd better go away, Roy. You haven't any right to say such things. (Tearfully.) Lon's going to be my husband . . . and I love him . . . and you're just jealous and mean 'cause I don't want you—'cause I never wanted you!

Roy has no answer. Her words have gone right through his heart. He looks at her for a moment, turns, and exits. Pard follows at his heels. Marie goes to door.

PA (to Marie):
I'm sure sorry.

MARIE (softly):
It's all right, Pa . . . Maybe it's just as well it happened this way.

She goes out. Velma is sobbing softly in Lon's embrace.

LON (angrily):
Some nerve he had. (Manfully; to Velma.) If it wasn't for you, dear, I'd have punched him right in the nose.

DISSOLVE TO:

200. INT. CAR ROY, MARIE, PARD
Roy stares ahead in stony silence. Marie drives, steals a
glance at Roy from time to time.

MARIE (after pause):
Am I going right, Roy?

ROY (vacantly):
Yeah. Straight ahead. (Turns to her slowly.) You
shouldn't have come in there, Marie. It was tough
enough without you.

MARIE (simply):
I had to go in. You thought of her more than you did
me, and I wanted to know why.

ROY:
You wouldn't find the answer just now. She was—
she was like two different people.

MARIE (she knows it):
You don't love her any more, do you, Roy?

ROY (slowly):
No. And if you weren't sure of it, you wouldn't ask
me.

DISSOLVE TO:

201.–206. OMITTED
These scenes have already been shot.

207. CLOSE-UP THE SHOE BOX
as a hand pokes around among the jewels.

CAMERA PULLS BACK TO:

208. MED. CLOSE SHOT ROY AND ART
Art is a little man with a wise, sharp face. As he continues
to poke the jewels, the little man's eyes get bigger and
bigger.

ART:
If I didn't know where they come from, I'd think they
was phonies.

146

ROY:

Poor old Mac. Too bad he couldn't have lived to see the stuff. (Shaking his head.) There he was, laying dead, and a half million bucks beside him. (Coming out of it.) Well, it's all yours now and I want my end.

ART:

You're goin' to have to wait a few days for that, Roy.

ROY (scowling):
What's that?

ART (shrugging):
Me—I'm strictly petit [petty] larceny with a cheap cut-in, but Larry's flying out here from Kansas City. I guess you know it's Larry that's got the dough in this caper. Mac was workin' for him . . . You leave the stuff with me and lam. But stick around close. (Pauses.) I can help you out a little, Earle, but fifty's my limit.

209.   CLOSE SHOT (SHOOTING OVER ART'S SHOULDER)   ROY

ROY:

You wouldn't pull a fast one on me, would you, Art? I don't like fast ones.

210.   MED. CLOSE SHOT   ROY AND ART

ART (nervously):
Take the stuff with you, if you feel that way. But it'll be like carrying a bomb around.

ROY:

Give me a hundred bucks. You keep the stuff. But if I don't get my end I'll come gunnin' for you and Larry, too. He ain't too big for me.

ART:

All right. A hundred it is.

He takes out his billfold and starts counting out bills. Roy picks up the bills, puts them into his pants' pocket, then he rises, hesitates, and begins to finger the jewelry. Art looks on without comment. Finally Roy selects a ring.

211.   CLOSE-UP   RING

in Roy's fingers. An unpretentious platinum ring with a medium-sized diamond set in it.

ROY'S VOICE (OVER SCENE):
That's the one I want. A copper could see some of them headlights fifty feet away but he wouldn't take a second look at this one.

212.   INT. CAR   CLOSE SHOT   MARIE   DAY

smoking a cigarette. Pard is asleep in her lap. OVER SCENE the SOUND of the surf pounding at the pier. In the background, closed beach concessions. Marie's eyes are closed, but at the sound of approaching footsteps they open quickly. Roy gets into the car and without saying anything, takes her hand, slips the ring on her finger. Marie looks at the ring and her face lights up with joy.

MARIE:
Oh, Roy!

ROY (grinning):
Present.

Marie flings her arms around him and begins to cry. After a moment she looks again at her hand.

MARIE (slowly; looking at the ring):
Of course you'd put it on the wrong finger.

FADE IN

213.   EXT. CABIN   AUTO COURT   NIGHT
MED. CLOSE SHOT   ROY AND MARIE

sitting on the steps of their cabin, watching the cars zip by on the highway. It is a dark, moonless night. Pard wanders in and out of the picture during the entire scene.

Roy, smiling, talks in a low tone. He has grown a moustache and is wearing glasses.

ROY:

The air's got a kind of feel to it tonight like back home. If I'd shut my eyes it'd be a summer night in Indiana . . . Yep . . . mighty nice on summer nights back on the farm in the old days. We'd play "run-sheep-run" and the girl from across the road'd come over . . . Her name was Roma . . . Roma Stover. I dreamed about her one night, remember? She had this long yellow hair like . . . (his face lights up) like Velma. Yeah . . . (He pauses and stares.) That's it . . . Velma reminded me of her and me never having the faintest idea. How do you like that? I was thinking of marrying Velma and it was just because . . . That's a hot one . . . Yeah, it was Roma I was thinking about all the time . . . Roma Stover . . . and her dead over twenty years! (He stares into space.)

A pause. Marie, made uneasy, finally speaks:

MARIE:

How come you left the farm, Roy? You must of liked it there a lot the way you're always talking about it.

ROY:

I don't know. Wanted excitement, I guess . . . I went to Indianapolis and got a job, but I couldn't stand the boss. He rode everybody and they took it . . . but not me. One day I cooled him off and got canned. I got a belly full of bosses before I was through. Them guys like you to be meek and mild so they'll feel big. That was the trouble. I felt just as big as they did . . . bigger . . . even if they was the boss.

MARIE:

How'd you ever get mixed up in bank robbery and stuff?

ROY:

> I went back to work on the farm after a while. Lefty Jackson's brother, Angus, was working on another farm not far away. One day Lefty stopped in to see Angus. He just got out of stir. We had a lot of fun sitting around talking. I don't know . . . Pretty soon I was in with the mob.

Roy straightens suddenly, grabs at his side.

MARIE:

> It's hurting you.

ROY (through his teeth):

> Yeah . . . but it'll stop. It comes and goes. (Takes a deep breath.) Better now.

MARIE:

> Poor honey . . .

ROY:

> Lucky, you mean. If that slug had torn through a little nearer center, it would have been just too bad. Nope, I ain't kicking.

Marie has turned her face away. Roy is unaware of the effect his words are having on Marie.

MARIE:

> You'd be dead . . .

ROY:

> Maybe . . . Maybe . . . It takes a lot of shooting to finish some guys . . . like Lefty Jackson. I bet he had forty holes in him before he stopped kicking . . . a little guy, too. I seen his body at the morgue.

MARIE (terrified):

> Stop, Roy, stop . . . I don't want to hear . . .

ROY (surprised):

> What's the matter?

MARIE:

Hold me, Roy, hold me real tight!

He puts his arms around her, kisses her twice, then:

ROY:

What come over you all of a sudden?

MARIE:

I don't know . . . I just got scared . . . If it should happen to you . . . (Brokenly.) You're all I got, Roy.

ROY (pats her hand):

Don't you worry . . . nothing's going to happen to me now. In two or three days we'll have all that dough. Then we'll be sitting pretty.

Pard, sitting on the bottom step, barks sharply. OVER SCENE, the SOUND of steps and the figure of a man appears out of the darkness and comes toward them on the gravel walk. It is the owner of the auto court, a little man in his shirt-sleeves and open vest.

OWNER:

Evening, folks . . . Both your cabins okay?

ROY:

Everything's fine.

OWNER (points to Pard):

Is that dog housebroken?

ROY:

Yeah . . . he is.

OWNER:

People ain't supposed to have dogs in their cabins, but if he's housebroken . . .

ROY:

Don't you worry.

Pard growls at the retreating figure. Roy laughs.

ROY:

> Atta boy, Pard.

Roy pats him. Pard wags his tail, then growls into the darkness after the owner.[18]

FADE OUT

FADE IN

214.   INT. CABIN   MED. SHOT   DAY

Marie is sitting by the window holding Pard in her lap. She gets up quickly, goes to the door, opens it. Roy enters, puts down a newspaper. He looks tired.

MARIE:

> Well?

ROY:

> Same old song . . . Larry ain't showed yet. I'm going to run out of dough calling that guy Art long distance.

MARIE:

> You should have taken the money Velma's boyfriend offered you . . . four hundred bucks. But no—you got to be the big shot . . . "Think nothing of it" . . .that's what you said. (She laughs.) Sucker!

Marie picks up the newspaper, opens it, and gasps.

INSERT   NEWSPAPER HEADLINE

> $10,000 REWARD FOR TROPICO GUNMAN

MARIE'S VOICE (OVER SCENE):

> Roy!

ROY'S VOICE (OVER SCENE):

> Yeah . . . Don't look like things are ever gonna cool off . . .

BACK TO SCENE:

MARIE:

> You know what Algernon said about Pard here being bad luck.

ROY:

That's malarky.

MARIE:

Maybe it is and maybe it ain't.

ROY:

How could a poor little dog be the cause of it? That's just plain dumb . . .

MARIE:

Sometimes you get me crazy. You think when you say a thing, that's that. Nobody knows nothin' but you.

ROY:

Okay . . . Pard's to blame for everything . . . It's all Pard's fault . . . Have it your way.

MARIE:

I didn't say Pard was to blame. I only said there might be something—

ROY (interrupting):
Aw—shut up.

MARIE (flaring):
Don't you tell me to shut up—you . . .

Roy winces slightly, turns away from Marie to hide it. Anger goes out of Marie's face.

MARIE:

Roy, it's hurting you! You come right in here and let me change that dressing.

She puts her arm around him, helps him into the bedroom.

215.   INT. BEDROOM   MED. SHOT   ROY AND MARIE
Roy tries to control his face while Marie unbuttons his shirt.

MARIE:
> Poor honey!

216.   INT. BEDROOM   CLOSE SHOT   ROY AND MARIE
SHOOTING directly at Roy, Marie standing behind him starting to remove the dressing.

MARIE:
> It don't look so good, Roy. It's all red way up under your armpit. You got any fever?

ROY:
> I don't think so . . . maybe I have . . . I ought to go in and see Doc . . .

MARIE (quickly):
> No, you can't do that. They might kill you. You can't trust nobody . . . not even your friends. Ten thousand dollars is a lot of money.

ROY:
> You ought to turn me in and live easy for the rest of your life.

MARIE:
> Roy . . . don't say things like that . . . even in fun!

FADE OUT

FADE IN

217.   EXT. GAS STATION   DAY
as a boy on a bicycle comes up, takes a paper out of his bag, and hands it to the owner.

OWNER:
> Thanks, sonny.

PAN TO:

218.   INT. GAS STATION AT AUTO COURT
MED. SHOT   ROY   AT TELEPHONE
SHOOTING through the glass. Roy puts down the receiver, hurries out. CAMERA PANS with him to:

219. EXT. GAS STATION   AUTO COURT
      MED. SHOT   THE OWNER OF COURT
      who is raking gravel before the station. He turns at the
      sound of Roy's steps, leans on his rake.

OWNER:
      Morning, Mr. Collins.

ROY:
      Morning.

He goes on toward the cabin.

220. INT. ROY'S CABIN   MED. SHOT   MARIE
      feeding Pard. She looks up as Roy enters.

ROY:
      Baby! Our troubles are over!

MARIE (quickly):
      Did Larry get in?

ROY:
      Yeah. I told him I'd drive in tonight. They'll have my
      cut ready then. How's that?

MARIE:
      That's great. Then we can hit east where we'll be
      safe.

She throws her arms around him and kisses him.

ROY:
      And I was beginning to think that Art and Larry
      were giving me the old oil.[19] Boy, it's sure easy to be
      wrong in this world!

MARIE:
      Love me?

ROY:
      I sure do . . . You bet . . . Let's get started.

Marie runs to the closet, begins to pull out clothes. Pard
goes over to the door and scratches. Roy lets him out, then

picks up a suitcase that is standing in the corner, and puts it on the bed. Suddenly he straightens, grimaces, beads of sweat appear on his forehead. Marie, carrying clothes to the suitcase, sees his face.

MARIE:
Pains?

ROY:
Yeah.

MARIE:
Poor honey . . . ! I'll drive in.

ROY:
Nothing doing. Suppose we get a rumble!?

MARIE:
We won't. They're not even looking for you yet. And if they was, they wouldn't know you now.

ROY:
All the same, I'll drive . . . (Pauses.) The car needs gas. I'll get her filled up.

He goes out.

221.   EXT. CABIN   AUTO COURT   ROY, OWNER, AND PARD
As he is about to get into the car, he sees the owner of the court bending over, snapping his fingers at Pard, who stands a few feet further along. The owner holds a paper in his hand, rolled up.

222.   ANOTHER ANGLE OF COURT   PARD IN FOREGROUND

OWNER:
Nice little Pard!

Pard's tail wags. In three strides Roy is behind the man, who turns quickly and jumps sideways.

ROY:
I want to see you.

The little man puts the paper behind him.

OWNER:
> I . . . I'm busy . . . Got a lot to look after this morning. Nice dog you got, mister. I was just trying to make up with him.

ROY:
> What makes you think his name's Pard?

OWNER:
> Didn't I hear you call him that yesterday? Maybe I'm wrong.

ROY:
> Let me see that paper.

The little man hands it over. He is trembling. Roy opens the paper.

223. INSERT   NEWSPAPER PICTURE OF ROY EARLE
on front page. The caption reads:
> AMERICA'S NEW PUBLIC
> ENEMY NO. 1

It is an old Bertillon picture of a leaner, stronger, more formidable Roy Earle.

224. TWO SHOT   ROY AND OWNER

ROY (jostles him toward the cabin):
> Come along.

225. INT. CABIN   MED. SHOT
Marie is just closing the suitcase as Roy and the owner enter. She glances up just as Roy jerks the .45 out of the waistband of his pants, looks on unbelievingly at what follows:

ROY:
> You know who I am, don't you?

OWNER:

No . . . I never saw you before . . . not until you came here . . . Honest.

ROY:

What you so scared about then?

The man holds his hand out in front of him as if to ward off a blow.

OWNER:

Please, Mr. Earle, don't kill me.

ROY:

Looking for that reward, huh?

He hits the man, who falls heavily. Roy opens the newspaper, reads:

INSERT   NEWSPAPER

"And believe it or not, he's traveling with a woman who answers to the name of Marie and a little white mongrel dog who answers to the name of Pard."

BACK TO SCENE:

MARIE (voice choked):
Mendoza!

ROY:

Yeah . . . He squawked. I should have taken care of him when he followed us out. (Reading again.) "Assistant District Attorney Small suspected Mendoza from the start and by playing on the vanity of this small timer, who wanted to be a big shot," . . . Look at the name they hung on me—"Mad Dog Roy Earle." Them newspaper rats!

MARIE:

What are we going to do, Roy?

ROY:

Marie, I got to park you like you said.

MARIE:

Like who said?

ROY:

Remember? We agreed when the going got too tough, I could park you. You said it was a deal.

MARIE:

I can't leave you, Roy. I don't care what happens to me. Let's stay together. Let the money go, Roy. Forget about it. We'll hit east. We'll make it. Then you'll be safe.

ROY:

It takes dough to get back east. We'd end up by heisting filling stations like a couple of high school kids. I got maybe ten grand coming to me and I'm going to get it. Listen, I got an idea. I'll put you on the Las Vegas bus. You can wait there for me. I'll go in and get my end . . . then I'll come after you and we'll hit east.

MARIE:

No, Roy, no! Don't leave me. I'm scared!

ROY:

Do you think I'm going to drag you in with me and get you shot? Brother, when they hang that Number One tag on you, they shoot first and argue afterwards. I know. "Mad Dog Earle." How do you like that? (Looks in the paper again.) Mendoza sure spilled everything. They'll hang the Kranmer killing on me if they get me—but they're not gonna get me. I've done all the time I'll ever do. I've seen them poor so-and-so's in the death cells . . . not for me.

MARIE:

What do you mean, Roy?

ROY:

I mean they'll never take me. That's what I mean . . .

The man on the floor groans. He's coming to.

ROY (continuing):
> You run down to that store on the corner and get a big basket with a lid on it. We'll put Pard in it—you take him with you.

MARIE:
> All right, Roy, I'll do anything you say.

ROY (motioning to owner):
> I'll tie him up and stick him in that closet so we can get a good head start . . . Hurry.

DISSOLVE TO:

226.   FULL SHOT   CORNER OF PAVED ROAD
lined with orange trees. Some twenty yards off a woman stands. The Buick pulls into the picture.

227.   CLOSE SHOT   ROY AND MARIE   IN CAR
Roy reaches in the back seat, takes out a wicker basket, opens it, lifts Pard in.

ROY:
> Lie down, Pard.

Pard obeys. Roy pats him, then covers the basket.

ROY (to Marie):
> Virge's Pool Hall . . . you can't miss it. Don't ask where it is, look for it. Just mention Art, and Virge will look after you. I'll be with you tomorrow night at the latest. Got that?

Marie nods, then she leans against Roy, begins to cry.

MARIE:
> I just got a feeling . . . Roy, please take me with you. I can't stand to be alone any more . . . I . . .

Roy frowns, compresses his lips, then shakes himself.

ROY:
> Can't be done.

MARIE (nods, after a pause):
I know . . . I'm sorry, Roy, for the way I've acted.

ROY:
You got nothing to be sorry about.

MARIE:
Yes, I have . . . nagging at you and flying off the handle. I wish I hadn't . . .

ROY:
I like it. I mean, that's the way married people act. My pa and ma fought like cats and dogs goin' on forty years . . . I wouldn't give two cents for a dame without a temper.

MARIE (sobs):
Oh, Roy . . .

The woman in the background starts moving out onto the road.

ROY:
The bus must be coming. (He reaches into his pocket, takes out a roll of bills.) Here, take this. (Hands the money to Marie.)

Bending down he kisses her but pulls away when she clings to him. Her face is pale, her lips twitching.

MARIE:
You're all I got in the world.

ROY:
Come on, kid . . . See you tomorrow night.

They get out of the car.

228. MED. SHOT ROY AND MARIE
Roy carries the suitcase in one hand and the basket in the other. He walks so fast Marie has to run to keep up with him. The bus comes into scene, stops with a squealing of brakes and the big door flies open.

DRIVER (calls):
> Make it snappy!

Roy puts the suitcase and basket inside first, then helps Marie.

MARIE (as the door closes):
> Good-by . . . Good-by!

Through the glass Roy sees Marie's pale, tear-stained face. The bus goes into gear, starts off. Roy stands looking after it until it is out of sight. Suddenly his face is distorted. PAN with Roy as he turns and runs toward his car.

229.   MED. SHOT   ROY'S CAR
as he gets in, starts the motor and makes a sharp U-turn, then starts to drive after the bus.

230.   CLOSE SHOT   ROY'S CAR
He has gone only a few hundred feet when a siren SOUNDS beside the car. Roy takes his foot off the gas. A motorcycle cop draws up alongside and motions him to the curb.

231.   CLOSE-UP   ROY'S HAND
as he unbuttons his vest, sets his .45.

232.   INT. CAR   MED. SHOT   ROY
He stops the car, looks back. The cop kicks the stand under his motorcycle, then pushes his hat back on his head, mops his brow, and comes forward.

233.   CLOSE SHOT   ROY AND COP

COP:
> Out of state, huh?

ROY (grinning):
> Yeah. What's wrong?

COP:
> Didn't you see that twenty-five-mile zone sign back there?

ROY:

>Sorry, I didn't.

COP:

>And you was sure stepping on it.

ROY:

>Was I? I didn't know it.

The cop takes off his cap and scratches his head. He is disarmed by Roy's attitude, which is one of contrite friendliness. The cop's face is haggard and sags with fatigue.

COP:

>I ought to give you a citation, but since you're from out of state . . . Boy, I been up all night and I'm tired.

ROY:

>Yeah?

COP:

>Yeah. And I got to stick on the job till relieved. Orders. Every policeman in Southern Cal's out looking for that Earle guy. He's either trying to get to L.A. or he's trying to get east. We got the main highways policed both ways. We'll get him. But it's tough on the boys. Some of 'em are fit to be tied, staying up all night. So watch your step, buddy, *watch your step.*

ROY (with a certain grim humor):
>Thanks for the tip, officer.

He waves his hand at the cop, starts up.

234.   INT. CAR   TRUCKING SHOT   ROY
He drives slowly until the cop passes on motorcycle. Then Roy pulls over to side of road, stops.

235.   INT. CAR   CLOSE SHOT
Roy takes out a road map, opens it, studies it.

236.   INSERT   ROAD MAP
as his fingers trace the route to Cajon Pass.

BACK TO SCENE:
Roy is scowling. He fishes in his pocket, takes out a crumpled dollar bill and some change, looks at the gas gauge.

237.   INSERT   GAS GAUGE
It registers three-quarters full.

238.   CLOSE-UP   ROY
frowning.[20]

DISSOLVE TO:

239.   LONG SHOT   HIGHWAY   THROUGH THE PASS
bordered by gentle hills beyond which rise the shapes of mountains dominated by the mountain. Fleecy clouds cast shadows which dapple the landscape. Along the highway the Buick moves from left to right.

240.   INT.CAR   (PROCESS)   CLOSE SHOT   ROY
He looks at the gas gauge, frowns.

241.   INSERT   GAS GAUGE
It registers about two gallons.

242.   CLOSE-UP   ROY
frowning.

243.   LONG SHOT   ROAD   SHOOTING THROUGH WINDSHIELD
over Roy's shoulder. The car enters a little town. He comes to the crossroad, which is the center of the town. Roy's car turns the corner, stops. He takes the .45 out of the waistband of his trousers, examines it, then puts it back, gets out of the car.

244.   EXT. DRUGSTORE
as Roy enters the picture. He pauses momentarily in front of the drugstore, lights a cigarette. Through the window we see the druggist standing behind the cigar counter reading a magazine. Roy enters the store.

245.   INT. DRUGSTORE
Roy enters in foreground and stands with his back to
CAMERA.

DRUGGIST (looking up):
    Can I help you, mister?

ROY:
    Yeah—cigarettes.

He points to the brand. The druggist reaches below the
counter for the cigarettes. As he does so, Roy's right hand
goes to his gun, which is hidden from CAMERA. The
druggist comes up with the cigarettes, stares.

ROY:
    Don't give me no trouble and you won't get hurt.
    Hand me the dough in the cash register.

DRUGGIST:
    Yes, sir. Don't get nervous with that gun. I'll never
    get myself shot up over money. (Turns to the cash
    register, rings it, and begins taking out bills.)

ROY:
    Got a sack?

DRUGGIST:
    Yes, sir, here you are. That's all there is except for
    pennies. I take it you don't want pennies.

Roy takes the sack, stuffs it into his pocket.

ROY:
    You're right . . . you got sense.

The druggist looks him in the eye. Suddenly he seems to
wilt. A look of horrified recognition comes over his face.
Roy backs away from him toward CAMERA.

246.   INT. DRUGSTORE   FULL SHOT
A big fat man with a badge on his shirt enters, looks from
the druggist to Roy.

MAN:
> What's the matter, John? What's goin' on here?

Roy is covering them both but the fat man is not afraid. He takes a step toward Roy.

DRUGGIST (cries):
> No, Tom, don't . . . let him alone . . . let him go . . . that's Roy Earle!

The fat man hesitates. Roy hits him with his left fist and the man goes down. Roy steps over him and makes a break for the street.

247.   EXT. STREET   PAN SHOT OF ROY
as he runs to his car. OVER SCENE a shot. Roy jumps into the car, makes a wild U-turn, and swings out onto the highway, his tires screeching.

248.   INT. DRUGSTORE   FULL SHOT
It is rapidly filling with people.

AD LIBS:
> How much did he get? Holdup, you say? Anybody shot?

TOM:
> I'da grabbed him but when you yelled Roy Earle, my legs got kinda weak.

OVER SCENE the SOUND of a motorcycle. A highway patrol officer pushes through the jam.

OFFICER:
> What is all this?

TOM:
> Holdup, Henry. A feller took John here for about thirty bucks. (Laughs.) John thought the feller was Roy Earle . . . You're plumb crazy, John. Why Earle's got half a million dollars worth of jewelry with him. What would he be holding up a drugstore for?

JOHN (sheepishly):
Sure looked like Roy Earle's picture.

OFFICER:
Which way did he go?

Several people motion.

AD LIBS:
That way . . . North . . .

OFFICER:
Went north, did he? Well, we'll take no chances. If it's Earle, he's trying to get back to L.A. over the pass at Bluejay. We'll get him. I'm going to use your phone, John.

249. LONG SHOT   THE SUMMIT OF THE MOUNTAIN
in the distance.

CAMERA PANS DOWN TO:

250. LONG SHOT   ROY'S CAR

251. CLOSE SHOT   ROY
driving. The grade is getting steeper, and now and then he shifts into second gear.

251A. CLOSE SHOT   WHEELS OF THE CAR
as they race along.

DISSOLVE TO:

251B. INT. BAUGHMAN LIVING ROOM   MED. SHOT
PA, MA, VELMA, MRS. BAUGHMAN, BAUGHMAN
Pages of newspaper are strewn all over the floor. Velma's mother is lying on the couch, a wet towel on her forehead. Baughman sits beside her, and from time to time throughout scene he freshens the towel in a pan of water. Ma is darning socks, her face expressionless while her fingers nimbly manipulate the needle. Velma sits stunned. Pa walks around the room hemming and hawing. He carries an open newspaper.

MRS. BAUGHMAN (hysterically):
I'll never get over it . . . ! That awful man in this house . . . ! Imagine . . . they call him a mad dog!

PA:
It's him all right . . . Yes, sir, at first I couldn't quite . . . but it's him . . .

MA (in an unnaturally calm voice):
A person has to be so careful nowadays.

VELMA:
The little dog, too. What did it say his name was?

PA (consulting paper):
Pard.

MA:
Some good in him or he wouldn't be carrying a little dog around, would he?

PA (explodes):
Some good in him! (Raises the paper, shakes it.) Look what he done for Velma!

MRS. BAUGHMAN:
He wanted Velma, that's all, and he didn't want her with a lame foot . . . I guess he must have plenty of money. He ought to, robbing people of five thousand dollars that way!

PA (shouts impatiently):
Five *hundred* thousand dollars, you mean!

BAUGHMAN:
Yeah . . . No matter what anybody says, Roy Earle's a big shot. (With considerable pride.) And he was right here in this living room!

MRS. BAUGHMAN (cries):
Oh, you fool! You fool!

The front door bursts open and Lon Preiser dashes in, his hat on the back of his head and a crumpled newspaper in his hand. He looks about wildly.

LON:
Look! It says in the paper . . . It's that man! I know it is!

VELMA:
Yes, it is.

MA:
We didn't know what he was at the time.

Lon sits down beside Velma, puts his arm around her.

LON:
Only think . . .

VELMA:
Feel how cold my hands are.

LON (takes her hands, holds them):
People . . . We must never say a word about this to anybody. We never heard of him. You know how things are back in Barrowville. (Leans over, kisses Velma on the cheek.) Just think . . . I almost gave him back that four hundred dollars! I'm glad I didn't . . . a thief like that!

Pa, at a window, turns, looks at Lon, is about to remonstrate. He changes his mind, shrugs, looks back out of the window.

PA (to himself, thoughtfully):
A thief like that . . . [21]

DISSOLVE TO:

252.   THE WHEELS OF THE CAR
CAMERA PULLS BACK, PANS with the car as Roy navigates a sharp turn in the road.

253.   CLOSE SHOT   ROY
driving. His face grim. His lips are compressed and his
jaw muscles are standing out.

254.   LONG SHOT   SHOOTING THROUGH WINDSHIELD
over Roy's shoulder. The car makes another turn in the
road.

255.   OMITTED

256.   CLOSE-UP   ROY
driving. His expression becomes suddenly intent. OVER
SCENE the SOUND of the siren whines faintly. Roy scowls,
then the scowl fades.

    ROY (grimly, to himself):
        Here it comes.

257.   MED. SHOT   THE CAR
The road is steeper. OVER SCENE the SOUND of the siren,
louder than before.

258.   CLOSE SHOT   THE TURNING WHEEL
in soft earth.

259.   CLOSE SHOT   ROY
driving. The car bucks, shudders, then lunges ahead.

260.   MED. PAN SHOT   THE CAR
as it stalls. Roy goes into reverse, backs a few yards, tries
it again.

261.   THE WHEELS
as the car stalls. OVER SCENE the SOUND of the siren always
louder.

262.   CLOSE   ROY   AT WHEEL OF CAR
He sits quietly for a moment, looks at the country around.
Then he sighs, gets out of car. He reaches in back of seat,

draws out gun case we saw in previous scene, high-powered repeating rifle, and fills his pockets with ammuni-
tion. Then he turns and surveys the country again. His
eyes fix themselves on a high point. (NOTE: In this and
subsequent action, we never actually see the machine gun
in action.)

263.   LONG SHOT   A BEETLING BLACK ROCK
jutting out from the white side of a mountain several
hundred feet up. A big crack runs through the rock.

264.   PAN SHOT   ROY
as he starts up the road carrying the rifle and gun case.
He leaves the road and begins to climb. CAMERA HOLDS
on him until he disappears around a turn. TROLLEY with
Roy climbing slowly. Once he stops and grabs at his side.
OVER SCENE the SOUND of motors.

265.   CLOSE SHOT   A BIG ROCK
as Roy climbs into the picture, sits down, the gun case
beside him, the rifle in his lap. He remains quiet until he
has caught his breath. OVER SCENE the SOUND of the motors becomes louder and then stops. Roy can hear the
voices of men.

266.   MED. SHOT   THE DEPUTIES' CAR
County police officers are milling about, preparatory to
taking up Roy's trail.

AD LIBS:
There's his tracks, let's go after him, boys . . . We
got him, but watch yourselves. Don't show yourselves to him unless you want to be shot up . . . Let's
go get him . . .
                                    CAMERA MOVES UP TO:

267.   PAN SHOT   THE MEN
as they start climbing the mountain following Roy's tracks.
OVER SCENE the violent stuttering of Roy's machine gun.

Its echoes roll from peak to peak, then die away. The men duck, lie close to the ground.

A DEPUTY'S VOICE (OVER SCENE):
Watch yourselves, boys . . . Machine gun!

268. PAN SHOT   ROY
as he climbs into the crack of the big rock, lies down. The machine gun case is open, but we do not see gun.

VOICE (shouts, OVER SCENE):
You—up there . . . you got no chance . . . We don't want to kill you . . . Come down . . . We won't do no shooting . . .

ROY (shouts):
Come get me, buddy . . . Come get me!

OVER SCENE the SOUND of the other motor getting louder and the voices of the men, their words indistinguishable.

ROY (shouts):
What's the matter . . . ? Yellow?

269. CLOSE SHOT   ROY
He lights a new cigarette from the old one and inhales deeply. The corners of his mouth turn up in a slight smile. OVER SCENE the SOUND of another car and voices calling. Roy puffs at his cigarette.

270. MED. SHOT   ROAD
A second carload has pulled up. Members of the first group of peace officers reenter the scene, talk with the newcomers. Most of the remarks are addressed to the sheriff, a small man with an angular jaw and beetling eyebrows.

AD LIBS:
He means to put up a fight, sheriff . . . That's right . . . He's got a machine gun . . . Up there on a rock

> . . . Hard to get at . . . Guess he means to take a few
> of us with him . . .

SHERIFF:

> No use getting ourselves shot up, boys. He can't get
> away.

SECOND OFFICER:

> You mean, just wait.

SHERIFF:

> Sure . . . Why not? He'll have to come out sooner or
> later.

THIRD OFFICER:

> We might use dynamite . . . blow up that there rock.

SECOND OFFICER:

> It would take an awful lot of dynamite.

SHERIFF:

> All we gotta do is wait. Come dark, we can throw a
> searchlight up there . . . [22]

DISSOLVE TO:

271. EXT. BUS TERMINAL   SALTAN, CALIFORNIA   FULL SHOT
as the bus pulls in.

272. INT. BUS   CLOSE SHOT
A radio is going at a nearby cigar and magazine stand.
Marie, sitting in the bus, doesn't listen at first.

VOICE (over radio):

> His position puts him in command of several hundred
> feet of territory between him and the road. Natural
> rock formations shelter him from attacks above . . .
> It is some five hours now since Roy Earle took to
> cover on the rock and there is no indication on his
> part to surrender.

Marie starts violently.

VOICE (continuing):
> The road up the mountain is a jam of traffic. Spectators are coming from all over. As I said before, the scene is some sixty miles from Ballard.

MARIE (frenzied, to driver):
> I—I must go back the way we just came. I—I forgot something.

DRIVER:
> That's okay with me, lady. (Motioning.) Return bus leaves from over there in about five minutes.

Marie picks up the basket, stumbles from the bus.

DRIVER (shrugs, to himself):
> Just like all dames . . . Don't know whether she's comin' or goin' . . .

DISSOLVE TO:

273. FULL SHOT   SIDE OF THE MOUNTAIN   NIGHT
A big campfire is burning in the road and men are crowded around it. The spotlights of several automobiles converge upon the rock. A couple of hundred feet down the road, flares have been lighted and a rope stretched. Peace officers are keeping back the crowd of sensation seekers. Hot dogs and peanuts are being sold.

274. MED. CLOSE SHOT   ROY
lying in the crack of the rock.

275. FULL SHOT   THE CAMPFIRE
surrounded by police officials, reporters, etc.

CAMERA MOVES UP TO:

276. MED. SHOT   SHERIFF AND DEPUTY

DEPUTY:
> How about turning all the spotlights out except one and then blink it every ten seconds, say, ten seconds on . . . ten seconds off. We could move up while the

light was out and find cover before it went on. How about trying that?

SHERIFF:

Too risky, If there was any chance of him getting away, I'd be for it but there ain't—so why run any risks? (He puffs at his pipe.) Say, I got an idea . . . Why, sure, it's just the thing . . . Funny, nobody thought of it before.

OFFICER:

What is it, sheriff?

SHERIFF:

Bill, you scout over to the ranger station, telephone town, and tell them to send us a high-powered rifle with a telescope sight.

BILL:

Sure thing . . .

He runs out of the circle.

AD LIBS:

Just the thing . . . You got the idea, sheriff . . . That'll do it.

SHERIFF (points):

Come daylight, we'll send a feller up yonder . . . some feller who can really shoot.

277. FULL SHOT   CROWD DOWN THE ROAD
A rope has been stretched across the road, and several peace officers are on guard. Lighted flares cast long shadows and give a ghostly look to the faces.

AD LIBS:

Sure is cold . . . Yeah, sure is . . . It oughta be, we're nine thousand feet up . . . Maybe Earle's frozen to death . . .

A man pushes through the crowd, climbs under the rope.

OFFICER:
> Hey, you . . .

MAN:
> It's all right, officer. I'm Healy of the *Bulletin*.

OFFICER:
> Let's see your police card.

Healy shows it to him. OVER SCENE the tut-tut of Roy's machine gun. Everybody turns, looks in the direction of the shooting, then:

AD LIBS:
> That's him, ain't it? Earle's machine gun . . . Brother, he ain't frozen to death . . . No, siree . . . [23]

278.   MED. CLOSE SHOT   MARIE   IN CROWD
She tries to take advantage of the moment to slip under the rope but the peace officer sees her.

OFFICER (grabs her arm):
> What's the idea, you? Get back where you belong. (He pushes her.)

She still has the basket with Pard inside.

OFFICER (to crowd):
> Anybody else tries that gets run in . . . see?

279.   CLOSE SHOT   MARIE
She puts down the basket, stands holding onto the rope for support. Her eyes are closed and her teeth are chattering.

CAMERA PANS TO:

280.   MED. CLOSE SHOT   HEALY
who is watching her. He frowns thoughtfully. He starts toward her.

281.   TWO SHOT   MARIE AND HEALY
as Healy comes into the picture.

HEALY:

> What were you up to, sister? Why did you want to get through the line?

She opens her eyes, looks at him. Her face is a mask of dull misery. She doesn't hear Healy's question.

HEALY:

> What did you mean to do?

OVER SCENE the SOUND of Pard's whine. Healy starts.

282. CLOSE-UP BASKET
at their feet.

283. TWO SHOT MARIE AND HEALY

HEALY:

> Cold, aren't you, sister? Come over here by the fire.

He tries to draw her away from the rope but she clings to it. Pard whines again.

HEALY:

> You got a little dog in that basket, haven't you, sister? A little white dog . . . ?

Marie's eyes become fearful. CAMERA PULLS BACK to include basket. As Healy stoops over, opens the basket, and Pard jumps out, Marie starts to cry.

HEALY:

> Boy, oh, boy!

The people in the crowd around are staring at Marie and Healy. The officer comes forward, goes toward them.

OFFICER (to Healy):

> What's the matter with *her*?

HEALY:

> Handcuff her, officer.

OFFICER (blankly):
What?

Healy whispers close to the officer's ear. The officer looks at Marie incredulously.

HEALY (sharply):
I'm *telling* you!

The officer reaches for his handcuffs.

DISSOLVE TO:

284. MED. SHOT   ROY   ON THE ROCK
SHOOTING from behind. The high points on the surrounding mountains reflect the light of the rising sun.

285. INT. CAR   MED. CLOSE SHOT   MARIE AND PARD
on the back seat. She is handcuffed to the rug rack. The sheriff stands with his foot on the running board. A group of men stand a little way off, watching.

SHERIFF:
Tell your man to come down and surrender peaceably. We don't want to kill him if we don't have to.

Marie makes no sign that she has heard.

SHERIFF:
Yell to him. Tell him he better put his gun away and come down. Do like I say if you don't want him killed.

MARIE (brokenly):
All right.

Marie raises her head, looks up toward the rock, begins to cry.

SHERIFF:
Go ahead . . . yell . . .

MARIE (suddenly, a fierce tone in her voice):
No . . . ! I won't . . .

SHERIFF:
>   What's that?

MARIE:
>   I won't . . .

SHERIFF:
>   We'll kill him . . .

MARIE:
>   He . . . he's got to die anyway. He'd rather it was this
>   way . . . (Sobs.) Go on . . . kill him.

SHERIFF (frowns):
>   Okay, sister. (Turns to the group of men.) All right,
>   Tim, do your stuff.

A tall, thin man in a mackinaw starts away from the group. He is carrying a rifle with a telescope sight.

286.   MED. CLOSE SHOT   ROY   IN THE ROCK
He is lighting a cigarette.

SHERIFF'S VOICE (OVER SCENE):
>   Earle, come down . . . this is your last chance!

ROY:
>   Come get me . . . There's plenty of you down there.
>   (Puts down rifle, reaches toward machine gun case.)

287.   MED. SHOT   CAR
Marie and Pard both heard Roy's voice. The little dog is leaping with excitement.

SHERIFF'S VOICE (OVER SCENE):
>   I tell you . . . it's your last chance!

ROY'S VOICE (OVER SCENE):
>   That's what you say, copper!

MARIE (moans):
>   Oh, Roy . . .

Pard jumps out of the car. CAMERA PANS with him as he runs up the side of the mountain. It's hard going for the little dog.

288.   CLOSE SHOT   ROY
dragging on his cigarette. Observing something out of scene, he leans forward, stares.

289.   MED. LONG SHOT   PARD
SHOOTING over Roy's shoulder, as he runs up the mountain.

ROY:
    Well, I'll be . . .

290.   CLOSE SHOT   ROY
scowling. Pard runs into scene, jumps to lick Roy's face in a frenzy of delight. Roy puts his hands on the dog to feel if he is real. Then he pushes him aside, gets to his feet, shouts:

ROY:
    Marie!

291.   CLOSE SHOT   TIM, THE MARKSMAN
as he puts his eye to the telescope sight of his rifle.

292.   LONG SHOT   ROY
through the telescope sight. The cross lines in the sight are on his middle. OVER SCENE the crash of the rifle. The recoil of the rifle throws Roy out of view.

293.   CLOSE-UP   ROY'S HAND
Pard comes into the picture, sniffs the fingers.
                             DISSOLVE TO:

294.   LONG SHOT   SHERIFF, DEPUTIES, REPORTERS
as they swarm up the mountain.

295.   CLOSE SHOT   HEALY, SHERIFF, AND LEADERS
of the group approaching. Suddenly they stop. Healy
starts slightly at what he sees, then controls his face.
Throughout his speech the SOUND of Pard's whining.

HEALY:

Big shot Earle! Well . . . Look at him lying there . . .
Ain't much, is he? His pants are torn, he's got on a
dirty undershirt. *Sic transit gloria mundi*—or something.[24]

FADE OUT

THE END

MARIE :
        WHAT DOES IT MEAN WHEN A MAN CRASHES OUT?

HEALY!
        IT MEANS HE'S FREE ~

Annotation to the Screenplay

1 In the film, a governor signs Roy's pardon, Wally picks up Roy at the prison, and Roy visits a park. The newspaper headline thus becomes a transitional device in the film, linking Roy in the park to Roy's meeting with Kranmer.

2 Tropico Springs probably signifies Palm Springs, California. See Ben Ray Redman, "A Ride to Remember," *Saturday Review*, March 30, 1940, p. 12.

3 In the film, the sign reads Shaw's Cabins, 4 miles.

4 The phrase "doing the book" is slang for serving a life sentence in prison.

5 None of the action or dialogue from scene 58 to this point is in the film.

6 In the film, the dialogue between Roy and Velma in scenes 86–89 contains references to a blue star and the planets Jupiter and Venus.

7 In the film, Pa's explanation is shortened, and Roy's reaction is expanded. Roy tells Pa that he seems to have known Velma for a million years.

8 In the film, Roy utters, in his sleep, phrases concerning "crashing out" and that "sweet Indiana farm." There is no mention of Roma.

9 Scenes 118–23 are not in the film.

10 The dialogue between Roy and Velma concerning dogs and reading habits is not in the film.

11 In the film, Velma is not as confused; she asserts that she wants to dance and have fun and that she doesn't love Roy at all.

12 In the film, the telegram begins, "Roy Collins: Shaw's Camp."

13 In the film, from this point until Mendoza demands to leave with them (in scene 170) only Roy's line "Heist 'em, buddy" is retained.

14 In the film, only the lines "He's taking the wrong road" and "Them coppers will go to the fire" remain from scenes 172–79.

15 There is no headline in the film.

16 The material from this point to the end of scene 189 is not in the film.

17 The material from this point to the end of scene 193 is not in the film. Instead, Roy tells Doc that he will go see Velma again.

18 Scene 213 is not in the film.

19 The phrase "old oil" has been replaced by "run around" in the film.

20 Scenes 229–38 are not in the film. Instead, Roy listens to a broadcast on his car radio describing the police dragnet.

21 Scene 251B is not in the film.

22 Scenes 252–70, in which the police chase Roy, are drastically altered in the film.

23 In the film, scenes 273–77 differ greatly from the screenplay. For example, a radio announcer reports on Roy's impending capture.

24 Scenes 294–95 are not in the film. Instead, after Healy notes that Earle "ain't much now," Marie asks, "What does it mean when a man crashes out?" Healy thinks that's an odd question, but tells Marie that "it means he's free." Marie walks toward and past the camera saying, "Free? Free!" The reporter does not say *"Sic transit gloria mundi"* in the film.

Production Credits

Executive Producer	Hal B. Wallis
Associate Producer	Mark Hellinger
Directed by	Raoul Walsh
Screenplay by	John Huston and W. R. Burnett
From a novel by	W. R. Burnett
Director of Photography	Tony Gaudio, A.S.C.
Art Director	Ted Smith
Dialogue Director	Irving Rapper
Film Editor	Jack Killifer
Gowns by	Milo Anderson
Sound by	Dolph Thomas
Special Effects by	Byron Haskin, A.S.C., and H. F. Koenekamp, A.S.C.
Make-up Artist	Perc Westmore
Music by	Adolph Deutsch
Musical Director	Leo F. Forbstein

Released: January 1941.
Running time: 1941 release, 100 minutes;
    1948 re-release, 96 minutes.

Cast

Marie Garson	Ida Lupino
Roy Earle	Humphrey Bogart
Babe Kozak	Alan Curtis
Red Hattery	Arthur Kennedy
Velma	Joan Leslie
Doc Banton	Henry Hull
Pa	Henry Travers
Healy	Jerome Cowan
Mrs. Baughman	Minna Gombell
Jack Kranmer	Barton MacLane
Ma	Elizabeth Risdon
Louis Mendoza	Cornel Wilde
Big Mac	Donald MacBride
Mr. Baughman	Paul Harvey
Blonde	Isabel Jewell
Algernon	Willie Best
Ed	Spencer Charters
Pfiffer	George Meeker
Art	Robert Strange
Lon Preiser	John Eldredge
Announcer	Sam Hayes
Auto court owner	Arthur Aylesworth
Sheriff	Wade Boteler
Wally	George Lloyd
Farmer	Erville Alderson
Fisherman	Carl Harbaugh
Shaw	Cliff Saum
Policeman	Eddy Chandler
Hotel guests	Charlotte Wynters and Louis Jean Heydt
Watchman	William Gould

Cast

Joe	Garry Owen
Margie	Dorothy Appleby
Bus driver	Eddie Acuff
Druggist	Harry Hayden
Pard	As portrayed by Zero

Inventory

The following materials from the Warner library of the Wisconsin Center for Film and Theater Research were used by Gomery in preparing *High Sierra* for the Wisconsin/Warner Bros. Screenplay Series:

W. R. Burnett, *High Sierra* (New York: Alfred A. Knopf, 1940), 292 pages.

Revised Final, by John Huston and W. R. Burnett, July 31, 1940, with changed pages to September 6, 1940, 142 pages.

DESIGNED BY GARY GORE
COMPOSED BY GRAPHIC COMPOSITION, INC.
ATHENS, GEORGIA
MANUFACTURED BY INTER-COLLEGIATE PRESS, INC.
SHAWNEE MISSION, KANSAS
TEXT AND DISPLAY LINES ARE SET IN PALATINO

Library of Congress Cataloging in Publication Data
Huston, John, 1906–
High Sierra.
(Wisconsin/Warner Bros. screenplay series)
Screenplay by John Huston and W. R. Burnett.
Original story by W. R. Burnett.
Includes bibliographical references.
I. Burnett, William Riley, 1899–
II. Gomery, Douglas.
III. Burnett, William Riley, 1899–   High Sierra.
IV. High Sierra. [Motion picture]   V. Series.
PN1997.H485   791.43'7   79–3961
ISBN 0–299–07930–9
ISBN 0–299–07934–1 pbk.

WW

The Wisconsin/Warner Bros. Screenplay Series, a product of the Warner Brothers Film Library, will enable film scholars, students, researchers, and aficionados to gain insights into individual American films in ways never before possible.

The Warner library was acquired in 1957 by the United Artists Corporation, which in turn donated it to the Wisconsin Center for Film and Theater Research in 1969. The massive library, housed in the State Historical Society of Wisconsin, contains eight hundred sound feature films, fifteen hundred short subjects, and nineteen thousand still negatives, as well as the legal files, press books, and screenplays of virtually every Warner film produced from 1930 until 1950. This rich treasure trove has made the University of Wisconsin one of the major centers for film research, attracting scholars from around the world. This series of published screenplays represents a creative use of the Warner library, both a boon to scholars and a tribute to United Artists.

Most published film scripts are literal transcriptions of finished films. The Wisconsin/Warner screenplays are primary source documents—the final shooting versions including revisions made during production. As such, they will explicate the art of screenwriting as film transcriptions cannot. They will help the user to understand the arts of directing and acting, as well as the other arts involved in the film-making process, in comparing these screen plays with the final films. (Films of the Warner library are available at modest rates from the United Artists nontheatrical rental library, United Artists/16 mm.)

From the eight hundred feature films in the library, the general editor and the editorial committee of the series have chosen those that have received critical recognition for their excellence of directing, screenwriting, and acting, films that are distinctive examples of their genre, those that have particular historical relevance, and some that are adaptations of well-known novels and plays. The researcher, instructor, or student can, in the judicious selection of individual volumes for close examination, gain a heightened appreciation and broad understanding of the American film and its historical role during this critical period.